Biology for Every Kid

Related Titles of Interest

The Thomas Edison Book of Easy and Incredible Experiments, by The Thomas Alva Edison Foundation

Chemistry for Every Kid: 101 Easy Experiments That Really Work, by Janice Pratt VanCleave

Nature for the Very Young: A Handbook of Indoor and Outdoor Activities, by Marcia Bowden

The Naturalist's Year: 24 Outdoor Explorations, by Scott Camazine

Biology for Every Kid

101 Easy Experiments that Really Work

Janice Pratt VanCleave

WILEY

John Wiley & Sons, Inc.

New York • Chichester • Brisbane • Toronto • Singapore

Illustrated by April Blair Stewart

Editing, Design, and Production: Publications Development Company, Crockett, Texas

The publisher and the author have made every reasonable effort to assure that the experiments and activities in this book are safe when conducted as instructed but assume no responsibility for any damage caused or sustained while performing the experiments or activities in *Biology for Every Kid*. Parents, guardians, and/or teachers should supervise young readers who undertake the experiments and activities in this book.

Library of Congress Cataloging-in-Publication Data

VanCleave, Janice Pratt.
  Biology for every kid : 101 easy experiments that really work /
Janice Pratt VanCleave.
     p. cm. — (Wiley science editions)
  Bibliography: p.
  ISBN 0-471-51048-3. — ISBN 0-471-50381-9 (pbk.)
  1. Biology—Experiments. I. Title. II. Series.
QH316.5.V36   1989
574—dc20   89-14790
                                                                            CIP

Printed in the United States of America

90 91 10 9 8 7 6 5 4 3 2

In memory of my son,
David Wade VanCleave (1962–1987)

Preface

Like its predecessors *Teaching the Fun of Physics* and *Chemistry for Every Kid,* this is a basic science experiment book designed to teach concepts, terminology, and laboratory methods. The 101 experiments featured in this volume were developed to demonstrate that biology is a part of our everyday life. All 101 experiments are unique in their ability to introduce biology concepts in a manner that makes learning exciting. These innovative experiments will introduce the world of biology to the young and old alike.

The introductory *Purpose* for each experiment gives the reader a clue as to the concept that will be introduced. The purpose is complete enough to present the goal, but does not give away the mystery of the results. There is an element of surprise in each and guaranteed fun.

Materials are needed, but in all the experiments the necessary items can be easily obtained. Most of the materials are readily available around the house. A list of the necessary supplies is included for each experiment.

Detailed step-by-step instructions are given, and every experiment is illustrated. Pre-testing of all the activities preceded the drafting of the instructions. *The experiments work.*

Expected results further direct the experimenter. This allows for an immediate positive reinforcement to the student who has performed the experiment properly and is corrective if the results are not achieved on the first attempt.

Another special feature of the book is the *Why?* section. A scientific explanation is given for each result. The best part is that this is done in terms that anyone can understand. The reader thus can acquire a useful collection of scientific facts, enjoyably, painlessly.

This book was written to provide young scientists with safe, workable experiments. Because of the accessibility of the supplies, all of the experiments can be successfully completed.

Above all, the objective of this book is to make the learning of biology a rewarding experience and, thus, encourage a desire to seek more knowledge about science.

Note:

The experiments and activities in this book should be performed with care and according to the instructions provided. Any person conducting a scientific experiment should read the instructions before beginning the experiment. An adult should supervise young readers who undertake the experiments and activities featured in this book. The publisher accepts no responsibility for any damage caused or sustained while performing the experiments or activities covered by this book.

Acknowledgments

I wish to express my appreciation to my children and their spouses, Ginger and Calvin, Russell and Ginger, and David and Tina, who gave me four grandchildren to help with the necessary pre-testing of each experiment. Thanks, Kimberly, Jennifer, Davin, and Lauren.

Many students have been involved in the pre-testing of these experiments since I used them as part of my teaching curriculum. I also present enrichment science classes for children, and the children perform the experiments that I write. These are some of the children that have helped with the pre-testing of the biology experiments in this book. I want to offer my thanks to them: Jeff, Cindy, and Jarrod Hogg; Douglas and Christi Culpepper; Sterling Russell; Robert and Kenneth Fleming; Allen and Krysti Witcher; Erin, Amber, and Ryan Pratt; Charlcie Rothband; Michelle Guenat; Craig Ray; Joel Scott; Christopher Christian; Randy Barnett; Anthony Curry; Wesley Sharp; Katie Collins; Kimberly Wilson; Kevin Quindlen; and Stanley Steed.

A note of gratitude to my friends, Janice and Charles Culpepper, Kay and Larry Hogg, Holly and David Ruiz, Nancy Rothband, Jo Nell Childs, Jacque Toland, Sandra

Kilpatrick, Joyce James, and Ruth Ethridge who help me to keep my life with Christ in order so that everything else falls into place.

My husband, Wade Russell VanCleave, deserves credit for any book I might complete. His support keeps me going, and it takes a very special person to live with a science teacher and author. He survives in a house with strange science experiments in various stages of development sitting everywhere. He is the light of my life and any accomplishments I make are due to him.

JVC

Contents

III. Experiments that Teach Us about Ourselves: The Amazing Human Body   143

Introduction

Biology is the study of the way living organisms behave and interact. The word biology originated from two Greek words, *bios* meaning life and *logos* meaning knowledge. This book deals with the study of the knowledge of life, biology. It focuses on three major areas—*botany,* the biology of plants; *zoology,* the biology of animals; and the biology of human beings. A foundation of basic biology facts can assist us in understanding not only ourselves, but our environment—the world around us. Knowing how plants grow can increase food productivity. Understanding cell functions leads to controlling diseases. This book won't help you discover the cure for cancer, but it will offer a key for opening doors leading to future scientific discoveries.

Biology took a giant step forward less than 400 years ago when Anton van Leeuwenhoek, a Dutch lens grinder, contributed to the perfection and use of the microscope. His curiosity about things led him to making more than 250 different microscopes. Each lens was designed to view a specific object. People visited his home to view through these specially mounted lenses the strange wiggling creatures that Leeuwenhoek called Wee Beasties. Elementary children today are able to see these organisms through an inexpensive handheld microscope. The electron microscope allows us to view cell parts that were not even dreamed of in Leeuwenhoek's day. Have we discovered it all? No. The more advanced the tools used, the more questions that arise. We build on the earned knowledge of generations of scientists. Our quest for solutions to mysteries and problems increases with each new discovery. Our knowledge of the universe is very limited, and there are so many questions still to be asked and answered. Even with our vast knowledge of biology there is much to be learned and discovered. Few clues are available as to how a simple plant uses water from the soil, carbon dioxide from the air and light energy from the sun to produce stored food, a process called photosynthesis. You will discover that there are many opportunities in the in the field of biology for a person with an inquisitive mind and a spirit of adventure. Much is yet to be learned, but great fun and excitement is in store for the beginning scientist in just discovering the biology secrets that have already been unlocked.

This book takes biology out of the professional laboratory and into your daily life experiences. All of the experiments in this book are basic enough for anyone not familiar with scientific terms to understand. It is designed to present technical biology theories in such a way that someone with little or no scientific training can interpret and understand. The experiments are selected on their ability to be explained very basically and on their lack of complexity. One of the main objectives of this book is to present the *fun* of biology. Not all 101 of the experiments are magical in nature, but they are found to stir the interest of young and old alike with the wonders and the fun of biology.

2

You will be rewarded with successful experiments if you read an experiment carefully, follow each step in order, and do *not* substitute equipment. It is suggested that the experiments within a group be performed in order. There is some build up of information from the first to the last, but any terms defined in a previous experiments can be found in the glossary. There is a standard pattern for each exercise:

1. Purpose: The basic goals for the experiment.
2. Materials: A list of necessary supplies.
3. Procedure: Step-by-step instructions on how to perform the experiment.
4. Results: An explanation stating exactly what is expected to happen. This is an immediate learning tool. If the expected results are achieved, the experimenter has an immediate positive reinforcement. A "foul-up" is also quickly recognized. The need to start over or make corrections will readily be apparent to you.
5. Why?: An explanation of why the results were achieved is described in terms understandable to the reader who may not be familiar with scientific terms.

General Instructions

1. *Read:* Read each experiment completely before starting.
2. *Collect Needed Supplies:* Less frustration and more fun will be experienced if all the necessary materials for the experiments are ready for instant use. You lose your train of thought when you have to stop and search for supplies.
3. *Experiment:* Do not rush through the experiment. Follow each step very carefully, never skip steps, and do not add your own. Safety is of utmost importance, and by reading

any experiment before starting, then following the instructions exactly, you can feel confident that no unexpected results will occur.

4. *Observe:* If your results are not the same as described in the experiment, carefully reread the instructions, and start over from step one.

Measurement Substitutions

Measuring quantities described in this book are intended to be those commonly used in every kitchen. When specific amounts are given, the reader needs to use a measuring instrument closest to the described amount. The quantities listed are not critical and a variation of very small amounts more or less will not alter the results.

The exchange between SI and English measurements will not be exact. A liter bottle can be substituted for a quart container even though there is a slight difference in their amounts. The list on page 5 is a substitution list and not an equivalent exchange.

English to SI Substitutions

English	SI (Metric)

LIQUID MEASUREMENTS

English	SI (Metric)
1 gallon	4 liters
1 quart	1 liter
1 pint	500 milliliters
1 cup (8 oz.)	250 milliliters
1 ounce	30 milliliters
1 tablespoon	15 milliliters
1 teaspoon	5 milliliters

LENGTH MEASUREMENTS

English	SI (Metric)
1 yard	1 meter
1 foot (12 inches)	$\frac{1}{3}$ meter
1 inch	2.54 centimeters

PRESSURE

English	SI (Metric)
14.7 pounds per square inch (PSI)	1 atmosphere

ABBREVIATIONS

atmosphere = atm
centimeter = cm
cup = c
gallon = gal.
pint = pt.
quart = qt.
ounce = oz.
tablespoon = T.
teaspoon = tsp.

liter = l
meter = m
millimeters = ml
yard = yd.
foot = ft.
inch = in.

I

Experiments for the Beginning Biologist

The World of Plants

A biologist is a person who studies about living organisms. People have been searching for thousands of years for the mysteries of life. Many of these mysteries have been revealed, but there is much yet to be learned.

Plants are living organisms, and there are more than 350,000 types of plants on the earth. People who choose to specifically study plants are called *botanists.* Botany, the study of plants, is a good starting point for learning about biology because plants and animals have basic similarities. The building blocks of life, cells, are in all life forms, plants as well as animals. Plants allow you to study functions that occur in all life forms.

Upon completion of Part I, you will be able to answer many questions relating to the needs of living organisms, their care, growth, and changes.

The material in this book barely scrapes the surface of known information about plants. These experiments were chosen to whet your appetite so that you will have a desire to study more about the wonderful carpet of plants that covers our world.

7

1. Spicy Escape

Purpose To demonstrate diffusion and osmosis.

Materials *eye dropper*
vanilla extract
balloon, use a small size
shoebox

Procedure

- *Place 15 drops of vanilla extract inside the deflated balloon. Be careful not to get any of the vanilla on the outside of the balloon.*
- *Inflate the balloon to a size that will comfortably fit inside the shoebox and tie the open end.*
- *Place the balloon in the empty shoebox. Leave the balloon in the closed box for one hour.*
- *Open the box and smell the air inside.*

Results The air smells like vanilla. The box is still dry.

Why? The balloon appears to be solid, but it actually has very small invisible holes all over its surface. The liquid vanilla molecules are too large to pass through the holes, but the molecules of vanilla vapor are smaller than the holes and pass through. The movement of the vapor through the rubber membrane is called *osmosis*.

The escaped vanilla vapor moves throughout the air in the shoebox. And once the shoebox is open, through the air in the room. This spontaneous movement of molecules from one place to another is called diffusion. If you wait long enough, the diffusion will result in a uniform mixture of the vanilla vapors and the air with which it mixes.

8

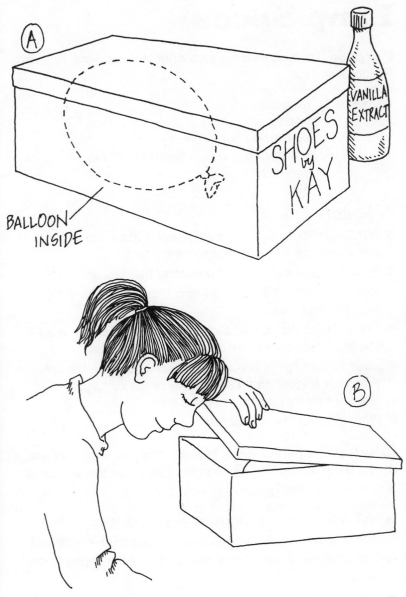

9

2. Limp Spuds

Purpose To demonstrate two critical conditions that influence osmosis.

Materials *table salt*
potato
measuring cup (250 ml)
measuring spoon —teaspoon (5 ml)
two small bowls
clock

Procedure

- *Mix 3 spoons of salt in 1 cup of water. Pour the salt water mixture into one of the small bowls.*
- *Pour 1 cup of water into the second bowl.*
- *Have an adult cut the potato into slices, about one-fourth inch (6 mm) thick.*
- *Place half of the potato slices into the bowl of water and the remaining slices into the bowl of salt water.*
- *After 15 minutes pick up potato slices from each bowl with your fingers and test their hardness or turgor pressure by trying to bend the slices.*
- *What differences do you feel?*

Results The potato slices in the water are very stiff and do not bend easily. The slices in the salt water are very limp and bend very easily.

Why? Two critical factors affecting osmosis are:
1. The amount of water and dissolved material inside the cell.
2. The amount of water and dissolved material outside the cell.

Osmosis is the movement of a material such as water across a membrane. Water always moves through a membrane toward the side containing the most dissolved material and the lesser amount of water. In this experiment, the dissolved material will be salt.

Salt and water are only two of the chemicals found inside all potatoes. The potato slices placed in the bowl of water keep the original amount of water in their cells plus more water from the bowl moves into the slices through cell membranes. This extra water makes the slices stiff.

The amount of salt inside each potato slice is less than that mixed with the water in the salt water mixture. The slices soaked in the salt water feel limp because they have lost some of the original water inside their cells. The water from inside each potato slice moves out of the potato through cell membranes and into the bowl of salt water. The slices are only partially filled and feel limp.

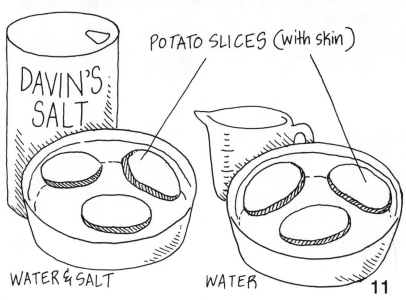

POTATO SLICES (with skin)

DAVIN'S SALT

WATER & SALT   WATER

3. Fluffy Raisins

Purpose To observe the effect of osmosis on a raisin.

Materials *glass of water*
10 to 12 raisins

Procedure
- *Place the raisins in the glass of water.*
- *Allow them to stand overnight.*

Results The raisins swell, become fluffy and smooth.

Why? During osmosis, water moves from a greater concentration through a membrane to an area of lesser water concentration. The raisins were dry inside, thus the water in the glass moved through the cell membranes into the raisins. As the cells filled with water, the raisins became plump and fluffy.

A

LAUREN'S
RAISINS

WATER

RAISINS

B

AFTER 24 HOURS

WATER

RAISINS

13

4. Stand Up

Purpose To demonstrate how the change in turgor pressure causes plant stems to wilt.

Materials *1 drinking glass*
wilted stalk of celery
blue food coloring

Procedure
- *Ask an adult to cut a slice from the bottom of a wilted celery stalk.*
- *Put enough food coloring into a glass half full of water to turn it dark blue.*
- *Allow the celery to stand overnight in the blue water.*

Results The celery leaves become a blue-green color, and the stalk is firm and crisp.

Why? A fresh cut across the bottom insures that the celery cells are not closed off or dried out. Water enters into the water-conducting tubes called xylem. These tubes run the length of the stalk of the celery. Water leaves the xylem tubes and enters the cells up and down the celery stalk. Plants usually stand erect and return to their original position when gently bent. This happens because each plant cell is normally full of water. The water makes each cell firm and all the cells together cause the plant to be rigid. A plant wilts when it is deprived of water and, like half-filled balloons, the cells collapse causing leaves and stems to droop. The pressure of the water inside the plant cell is called *turgor pressure.*

Living plants can take in water to produce pressure ranging from 60 to 150 pounds per square inch (4 to 10 atmospheres). The pressure becomes so great during rainy seasons that fruits and vegetables can burst. The pressure is enough for growing plants to move rocks and break through concrete.

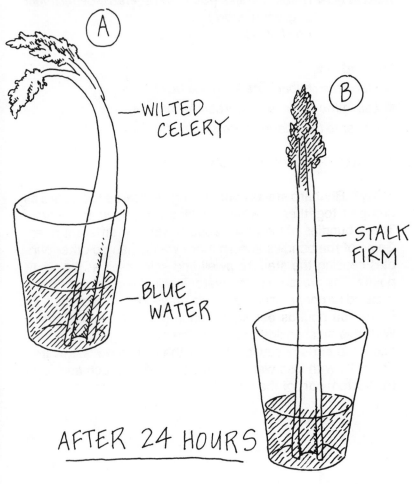

(A)

—WILTED CELERY

(B)

— STALK FIRM

—BLUE WATER

AFTER 24 HOURS

5. Curling

Purpose To determine what causes plants to burst when over watered.

Materials *rhubarb stalks (found in vegetable department of grocery store)*
bowl of water

Procedure

- *Place the rhubarb stalks in the bowl of water.*
- *Leave the stalks undisturbed for one day.*
- *Observe the shape of the stalks after being in the water.*

Results The ends of the stalks split and curl.

Why? Rhubarb stalks contain long vertical cells that are all grouped together in what is called *fibrovascular bundles.* These bundles of long cells absorb water at different rates. Some of the bundles absorb more water than do other bundles causing the stalk to swell and split apart at the weak points. The pressure of the water inside the cells of the stalk is called *turgor pressure,* and this pressure can be as high as 60 to 150 pounds per square inch (4 to 10 atmospheres). With this much inside pressure, the stalk of rhubarb bursts open and curls because some of the cells have less water. The cells with less water do not expand as much and form the bottom part of the curl.

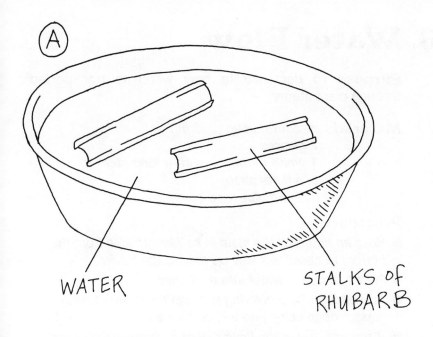

WATER

STALKS of
RHUBARB

RHUBARB

17

6. Water Flow

Purpose To demonstrate how water is transported through plant stems.

Materials *measuring cup (250 ml)*
2 glasses
1 white carnation with a long stem (purchase at a floral shop)
red and blue food coloring

Procedure

■ *Have an adult cut the stem in half lengthwise from the bottom to about half way up toward the flower.*

■ *Pour 1/2 cup of water into each glass.*

■ *Add enough food coloring to make the water in each glass a deep color, one will be blue and the other red.*

■ *Place one end of the flower stem in the blue water and the other end in the red water.*

■ *Leave the flower standing in the water for 48 hours.*

Results After 48 hours, the flower will have changed color. One side will be red and the other blue.

Why? Tiny tubes, called *xylem*, run up the stalk to the flower petals. The colored water moves through the xylem allowing the color to be distributed throughout the cells in the petals causing their color to change. Minerals in the soil are carried to plant cells in this way providing nutrients to the flowers and leaves. The minerals dissolve in water as did the red and blue coloring and the solution is carried up to the leaves and flowers where the dissolved material is left as was the red and blue dye.

18

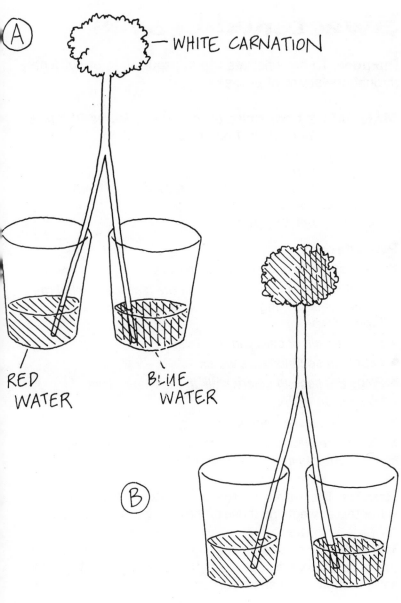

Ⓐ ——WHITE CARNATION

RED
WATER

BLUE
WATER

Ⓑ

19

7. Sweetened Leaves

Purpose To demonstrate the transportation of nutrients through the stems of plants.

Materials *2 fresh stalks of celery with leaves (the pale inner stalks from the bunch is best)*
2 glasses
sugar
measuring spoon—tablespoon (15 ml)
masking tape
marking pen

Procedure

- *Fill each glass one-half full with water.*
- *Add 4 spoons of sugar to one of the glasses —label the glass sweet making a label from a piece of masking tape.*
- *Place a stalk of celery in the Sweet glass.*
- *Label the second glass water.*
- *Place the second celery stalk in the water glass.*
- *Wait for 48 hours.*
- *Taste the leaves from each celery stalk.*
- *Use the results of this experiment to help you to explain how nutrients in the soil reach the leaves of plants.*

Results The leaves on the celery standing in the sweet water taste sweet and those of the celery in the water do not.

Why? Water moves up the stems of plants through tiny tubes called xylem tubes. Anything small enough to dissolve in the water can be carried up the stem to the leaves.

20

Nutrients in the soil that are able to dissolve in ground water are transported by the water through the xylem tubes in the plant stem and out to the cells of each leaf.

Note: Never taste anything in a laboratory setting unless you are sure that there are no harmful chemicals or materials. Some plants have poisonous leaves. This experiment is safe since only celery and sugar are present.

8. Leaf Straw

Purpose To demonstrate that the leaves and stems of plants can act like a straw.

Materials *glass soda bottle*
ivy leaf and stem
clay
straw
pencil
mirror

Procedure

- *Fill the bottle to within an inch of its top.*
- *Wrap the clay around the stem near the leaf.*
- *Place the stem into the bottle. The end of the stem must be below the surface of the water.*
- *Cover the mouth of the bottle with the clay.*
- *Push the pencil through the clay to make an opening for the straw.*
- *Insert the straw so that its opening is in the air space at the top of the bottle.*
- *Squeeze the clay around the straw.*
- *Stand in front of the mirror and look at the mirror image of the bottle while you suck the air out of the bottle through the straw. This should be difficult if there are no leaks in the clay so use a lot of suction.*

Results Bubbles start forming at the bottom of the stem.

Why? There are holes in the leaf called *stomata*, and tiny tubes called *xylem* run down the stem. The leaf and stem acted like a straw. As you sucked air out of the straw more was drawn in through the leaf straw. It is through these tubes and holes that water moves in a plant.

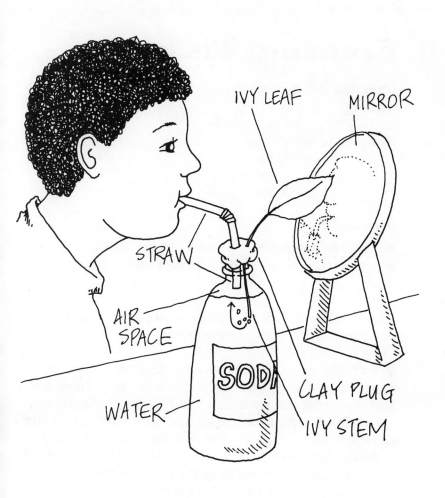

IVY LEAF

MIRROR

STRAW

AIR SPACE

SODA

CLAY PLUG

IVY STEM

WATER

23

9. Freezing Tissue

Purpose To determine how leaf structure affects its freezing.

Materials *lettuce leaf*
celery leaf
green onion
paper towel

Procedure
- *Place the vegetables in a freezer on the paper towel.*
- *Check them every 2 minutes to determine which freezes first.*

Results The lettuce and celery leaves froze first and the onion took a much longer time to freeze.

Why? There are several reasons for these results. One reason is that the vegetables with the largest surface area lose heat more quickly. When you consider that small garden plants except for onions all have leaves with about the same surface area, then other factors must be considered to explain their rate of freezing. See Experiment 10 *Hard to Freeze* to discover how the amount of nutrients in the cell fluid affects the freezing rate of the plant.

24

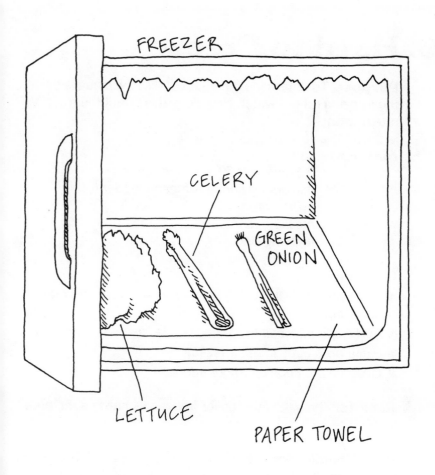

FREEZER

CELERY

GREEN
ONION

LETTUCE

PAPER TOWEL

25

10. Hard to Freeze

Purpose To determine the effect of dissolved nutrients on the freezing rate of water. How does this affect the freezing rate of plants?

Materials *salt*
2 5-ounce (150 ml) paper cups
measuring spoon —teaspoon (5 ml)
refrigerator
masking tape
marking pen

Procedure

- *Fill both cups with water, label one salt-water and the other water.*
- *Add 1 spoon of salt to the cup labeled salt-water and stir.*
- *Place both cups in the freezer.*
- *Observe the cups at 2-hour intervals.*

Results The salt water never freezes as hard as the pure water.

Why? Salt lowers the freezing point of water. The pure water was able to freeze at a warmer temperature than the salty water. In Experiment 9 *Freezing Tissue,* vegetables were observed to freeze at different rates. Their surface area affects this, but it is also possible that the amount of dissolved nutrients in the cell fluid also affects their resistance to the cold. Farmers find that bean, cucumber, eggplant, peppers, squash, and tomato plants cannot stand even the lightest frost while plants like broccoli, brussel sprouts, cabbage, collards, mustard greens, radishes, and turnips can withstand heavy frosts. Some of these durable plants have large leaves which supports the idea that there is more to determining the freezing durability than just surface area. The materials dissolved in their leaves help to make them more frost resistant.

FREEZER

WATER

SALT + WATER

11. Food Producers

Purpose To demonstrate that starch, a food substance, is produced in leaves.

Materials *paper towels*
tincture of iodine
leaf, pale green
rubbing alcohol
shallow dish
pint (500 ml) jar with a lid
measuring cup (250 ml)

Procedure

■ *Place the pale green leaf in the jar. The paler the leaf, the easier it will be to extract the green pigment, chlorophyll.*

■ *Pour 1 cup of alcohol into the jar. Put the lid on the jar.*

■ *Allow the jar to stand for one day.*

■ *Remove the leaf and dry it by blotting with a paper towel.*

■ *Lay the leaf in the shallow dish.*

■ *Add enough iodine to cover the leaf.*

Results Dark areas appear on the leaf.

Why? Photosynthesis is an energy-producing reaction that occurs in the leaves of plants. Starch, a food substance, is one of the products of this reaction. Soaking the leaf in alcohol removes the waxy coating on the leaf plus it partially removes the green pigment, chlorophyll. It is easier to see the results of the starch test without the presence of the green chlorophyll. Iodine combines with starch particles to form a dark purple to black color.

A

RUSSELL'S
RUBBING
ALCOHOL

LEAF
ALCOHOL

B

EYEDROPPER

IODINE

LEAF

TINA'S
TINCTURE
OF
IODINE

PAPER TOWEL

29

12. What's Stomata?

Purpose To determine which side of the plant leaf takes in gases.

Materials *potted plant*
vaseline

Procedure
- *Coat the top of four leaves with a heavy layer of vaseline.*
- *Coat the underside of four leaves with a heavy layer of vaseline.*
- *Observe the leaves daily for one week.*
- *Is there any difference in the two sets of leaves?*

Results The leaves that had vaseline coated on the underside died. The other leaves remained unchanged.

Why? Openings on the underside of plant leaves called *stomata* allow gases to move into and out of the leaves. The vaseline plugged the openings and the leaf was not able to receive necessary carbon dioxide gas or eliminate excess oxygen gas.

A

JEFF'S VASELINE

B

31

13. Water Loss

Purpose To demonstrate transpiration, the loss of water from leaves.

Materials *growing plant*
plastic sandwich bag
tape (cellophane)

Procedure
- *Place the sandwich bag over one leaf.*
- *Secure the bag to the stem with the tape.*
- *Place the plant in sunlight for two to three hours.*
- *Observe the inside of the bag.*

Results Droplets of water collect on the inside of the plastic bag. The inside of the bag may appear cloudy due to the water in the air.

Why? Plants absorb water from the soil through their roots. This water moves up the stem to the leaves where 90 percent is lost through the pores of the leaf (stomata). Some trees lose as much as 15,000 pounds (6810 Kg) of water within a 12-hour period. Plants can greatly affect temperature and humidity of a heavily vegetated area. This loss of water through the stomata of the leaves is called *transpiration.*

A

TAPE

PLASTIC
BAG

—POTTED PLANT

B

33

14. Desert Plants

Purpose To demonstrate the rate of evaporation from different leaf structures.

Materials *3 paper towel sheets*
waxed paper
cookie baking sheet

Procedure

- *Dampen the paper towel sheets with water. They should be wet, but not dripping.*
- *Lay one paper towel flat on the baking sheet.*
- *Roll up a second paper towel and place it next to the flat one on the pan.*
- *Roll the last paper towel as you did the second one, but cover the outside of the roll with waxed paper.*
- *Secure the ends, top and bottom, of the waxed paper roll with paper clips.*
- *Place the waxed covered paper roll on the baking pan.*
- *Position the pan with its paper rolls where it will receive direct sunlight.*
- *Unroll the paper after 24 hours and feel the paper.*

Results The flat towel is dry. The rolled towel is dry on the ends, but has damp spots inside. The waxed paper coated towel is damp all over.

Why? The more surface area that is exposed to the air, the faster the water evaporates. The speed that the water evaporates is called the evaporation rate. Desert plants have thick and/or round leaves to help prevent water loss. The surface of the leaves is waxy, further restricting water loss. The shape, thickness, and covering of desert plant leaves causes them to have a very slow rate of evaporation.

34

FLAT
PAPER TOWEL

ROLLED
PAPER TOWEL

BAKING
PAN

WAX PAPER COVERED
ROLLED PAPER TOWEL

15. Plants Breathe

Purpose To demonstrate that plants as well as animals exhale carbon dioxide

Materials *distilled water*
1 quart (1 liter) of purple cabbage indicator (see preparation instructions below)
sprig of Elodea or other water plant (found at pet store)
3 pint (500 ml) jars with lids
straw
aluminum foil

Procedure
Making the Purple Cabbage Indicator

- *Cut a head of purple cabbage into small pieces. The leaves may be pulled off and torn into small pieces.*
- *Place the cabbage pieces in a two-quart bowl.*
- *Add enough hot distilled water to fill the bowl.*
- *Allow the cabbage to stand until the water cools.*
- *Discard the cabbage pieces and save the blue liquid.*

Showing that Plants Breathe

- *Rinse the jars with distilled water.*
- *Place the Elodea in one of the jars. Fill the jar with purple cabbage indicator.*
- *Put the lid on the jar and cover the outside of the jar with aluminum foil.*
- *Pour one-half of the remaining cabbage juice into a second jar. Close the lid, and cover the outside of the jar with aluminum foil. Position both jars so that they will not be disturbed for 2 days.*

36

- *Pour the remaining cabbage juice into the third jar.*
- *Use a straw to exhale into the solution until a color change occurs.*

Results The indicator with the plant and the one exhaled into both turn from blue to a reddish color. The third solution is unchanged.

Why? The indicator contains water and a dye extracted from the purple cabbage. Carbon dioxide from exhaled breath and from the plant combines with the water to form a weak acid called carbonic acid. The cabbage dye turns red when mixed with any acid. Plants produce oxygen by a process called photosynthesis. This requires sunlight. What do they do at night when there is no sun? It is in the dark that they use oxygen and food as do animals, to produce carbon dioxide, water, and energy. This is called *respiration.*

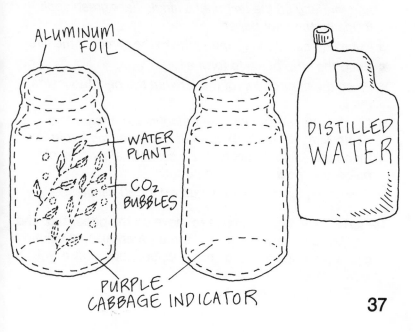

ALUMINUM
FOIL

WATER
PLANT

CO_2
BUBBLES

DISTILLED
WATER

PURPLE
CABBAGE INDICATOR

16. Leaf Colors

Purpose To separate and identify color pigments in leaves.

Materials *alcohol*
green leaf
coffee filter
pencil
baby food jar
ruler

Procedure

- *Place the leaf, top side down, on the edge of the coffee filter.*
- *Rub the pencil lead back and forth ten times over the leaf about one half inch (13 mm) from the edge of the paper.*
- *Rotate the leaf and repeat step two. Continue moving and marking on the leaf until a single dark green spot forms on the filter paper.*
- *Cut a one-half inch (13 mm) strip to the center of the filter.*
- *Bend the strip down to form a tab.*
- *Place the filter on top of the jar with the bent tab inside the jar.*
- *Lift the filter and slowly pour alcohol into the jar to a depth that allows the bottom of the paper tab to barely touch the liquid.* Important: *Be sure the alcohol level is below the green dot on the paper.*
- *Allow the paper to sit undisturbed for 30 minutes.*

Results The alcohol starts to move up the paper tab, and the green dot dissolves in it. As the green alcohol solution climbs up the paper, the green color stops and a yellow streak forms.

38

Why? Plants contain several color pigments that are necessary in the energy production reaction called photosynthesis. The green pigment is the most abundant, causing most plant leaves to appear green in color. Another pigment is present, but in smaller quantities. It is called carotenoid and ranges in color from red to yellow. Carotenoid is responsible for the color of fruits and flowers. The beautiful colors of fall leaves are due to the fact that chlorophyll stops being formed first, leaving carotenoid to display its colors.

Living things are composed of many different chemicals. You have just used the process called paper chromatography to separate and observe two of the many. Chromatography means "to write with color." The chemicals dissolve in the alcohol and move up the paper. The heavier material settles out first allowing separation of the lighter substances from the heavier ones.

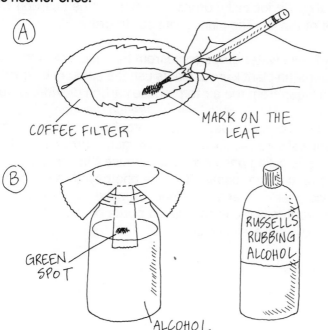

(A)

COFFEE FILTER

MARK ON THE
LEAF

(B)

GREEN
SPOT

RUSSELL'S
RUBBING
ALCOHOL

ALCOHOL

17. Independence

Purpose To demonstrate the independence of plants.

Materials *1-gallon (4-liter) jar with a large mouth and lid*
small pot plant

Procedure
- *Moisten the soil of the plant.*
- *Place the entire plant, pot and all, inside the gallon jar.*
- *Close the jar with its lid.*
- *Place the jar somewhere that receives sunlight for part of the day.*
- *Leave the jar closed for 30 days.*

Results Periodically, drops of water will be seen on the inside of the jar. The plant continues to grow.

Why? The water drops come from the moisture in the soil and from the plant leaves. Plants use the sugar in their cells plus oxygen from the air to produce carbon dioxide, water, and energy. This is called the *respiration* reaction. They can use the carbon dioxide, water, chlorophyll, and light energy in their cells to produce sugar, oxygen, and energy. This process is called *photosynthesis*. Notice that the products of the respiration reaction fuel the photosynthesis reaction and vice versa. Plants continue to make their own food. They eventually die in the closed bottle because the nutrients in the soil are used up.

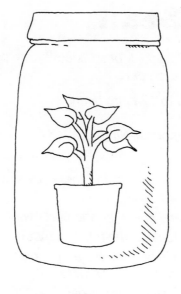

WATER DROPS

41

18. Baby Bean

Purpose To dissect a bean, identify the parts, and learn the function of each part.

Materials *10 to 12 pinto beans*
              jar
              paper toweling

Procedure

- *Inspect a dry bean and find these parts: micropyle, hilum, and seed coat.*
- *Place the beans in the jar and cover with water.*
- *Allow the jar to sit in the refrigerator overnight.*
- *Remove the beans from the jar and place on a paper towel to absorb the excess water.*
- *Carefully remove the coat from one of the beans.*
- *On the rounded side, pry the bean open with your fingernail. Be very gentle as you open the bean.*

Results What appears to be a baby bean is found inside the bean. If you do not find the baby plant or it was broken in the process of opening the bean, try again with another bean.

Why? The function of each bean part:

1. seed coat—protective covering
2. bean—food for the growing baby plant
3. micropyle—small opening through which pollen grains enter
4. hilum—where the bean was attached to the pod wall
5. epicotyl—forms the leaves
6. hypocotyl—forms the stem
7. radicle—forms the roots

42

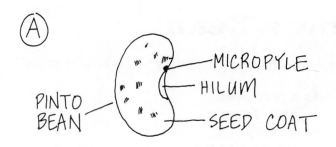

(A)

PINTO BEAN

MICROPYLE
HILUM
SEED COAT

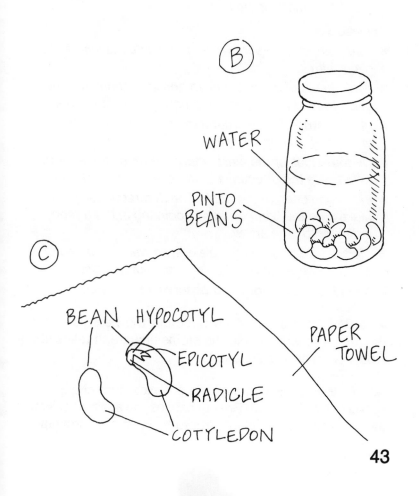

(B)

WATER

PINTO BEANS

(C)

BEAN HYPOCOTYL
EPICOTYL
RADICLE
COTYLEDON

PAPER TOWEL

43

19. Grow a Bean

Purpose To determine if it matters how seeds are planted.

Materials *4 pinto beans*
paper toweling
masking tape
one drinking glass
marking pen

Procedure

- *Fold a sheet of paper toweling, and line the inside of the glass with it.*
- *Wad sheets of paper toweling and stuff them into the glass to hold the paper lining tightly against the glass.*
- *Place a strip of tape around the outside of the glass about half way up the glass.*
- *On four sides of the glass, mark the tape with an arrow to indicate the directions of up, down, left, and right.*
- *Place one bean to the right of each directional arrow. Make sure the bean's hilum is pointing in the direction indicated by the arrow.*
- *Moisten the paper in the glass with water. You do not want the paper to be dripping wet—only moist.*
- *Keep the paper moist and observe for 7 days.*

Results No matter which direction the bean is planted, the roots grow down and the stems upward. It takes about 7 days for measurable results.

Why? Plants contain auxin, a chemical that changes the speed of plant growth. Gravity causes the auxin to collect in the lower part of the plant structure. Stem cells grow faster

44

on the side where there is more auxin causing the stem to bend upward. Root cells grow faster on the side where there is a smaller amount of auxin causing this section to bend downward. The end result is that auxin causes stems to grow up and roots to grow down.

Going Further Will these plants wind around an object? Will they wind in a specific direction? See Experiment 20 *Which Way?* to find out more about this.

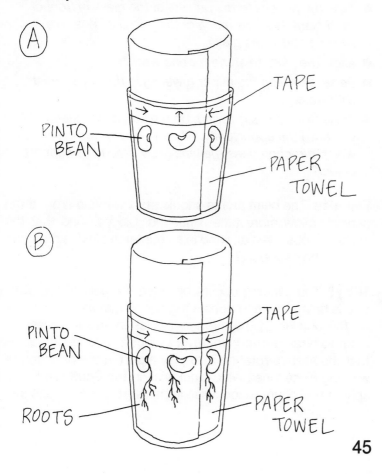

20. Which Way?

Purpose To determine the direction of winding plants.

Materials *glass of growing beans from Experiment 19*
4 pencils
masking tape

Procedure

- *Tape the pencils to the outside of the glass in front of each plant. Have as much of the pencil as possible sticking above the glass.*
- *Allow the plant to stand for one week.*
- *Be sure to keep the paper toweling in the glass moist with water.*
- *While the plant is growing, do a bit of field research if you have the opportunity. Observe any growing vine. In which direction does the vine grow around its support object?*

Results The bean stems should start winding around the pencils. Allow more time if needed. Did you find that the vines you observed all wind in a counterclockwise direction around their support?

Why? The winding occurs because the part of the stem that is being touched does not grow as fast as the outside. As the outside of the stem increases in size it forces the stem to wrap around whatever object it touches. It seems that the earth's rotation may play a part in the direction of winding since vines wind clockwise in the Southern Hemisphere and counterclockwise in the Northern Hemisphere.

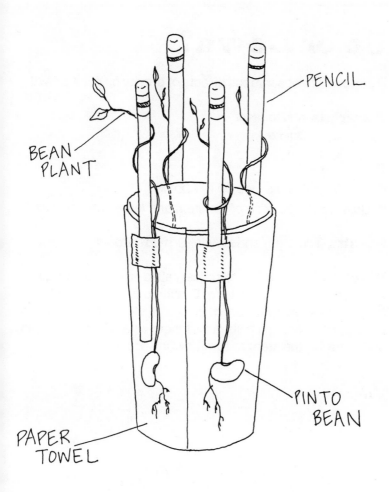

PENCIL

BEAN
PLANT

PINTO
BEAN

PAPER
TOWEL

47

21. Up or Down?

Purpose To observe the effects of gravity on plant growth.

Materials *house plant*
books

Procedure
- *Lay the pot on its side on the books.*
- *Observe the position of the stem and leaves for one week.*

Results The stem and leaves turn upward.

Why? Plants contain a chemical called auxin. Auxin causes plant cells to grow extra long. Gravity pulls the plant chemical downward so that along the bottom of the stem there is a build up of auxin. The cells grow longer where the auxin build up is causing the stem to turn upward.

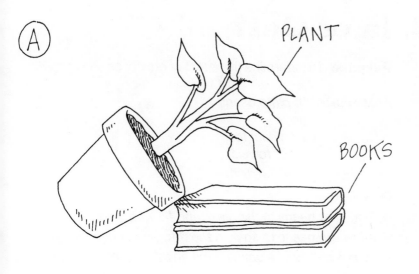

PLANT

BOOKS

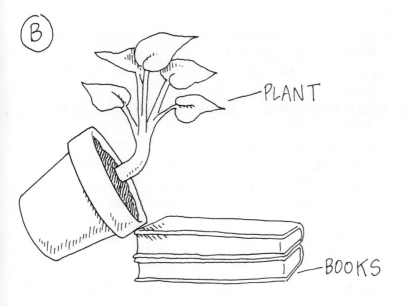

PLANT

BOOKS

22. In or Out?

Purpose To determine the effect of gravity on seed growth.

Materials *16 pinto beans*
glass
aluminum foil
paper towels
record player

Procedure

- *Place the beans in the glass and fill with water.*
- *Allow the beans to soak in the refrigerator overnight.*
- *Tear 4 pieces of aluminum foil about one-foot (30 cm) square.*
- *Place a paper towel in the center of each piece of foil.*
- *Moisten each paper towel with water. The towels are to be damp, not dripping wet.*
- *Place four soaked beans in the center of each paper towel.*
- *Fold the aluminum foil around the towel and close each end of the foil.*
- *Allow the foil containing the beans to stand for 3 days.*
- *Evenly space the 4 foil pieces on the turntable of the record player and turn it to 75 rpm.*
- *Allow the machine to rotate continuously for 5 days.*

Results The roots will grow outward and any leaves present will turn toward the center of the turntable.

Why? The rotating turntable produces a simulated field of gravity with an outward force that affects the root and

50

stem growth. This outward force pulls the plant-growth chemical auxin toward the outside of the machine. Stems grow away from auxin build up while roots grow toward it. More auxin builds up on the outer side of the bean causing the stems to grow inward and the roots outward.

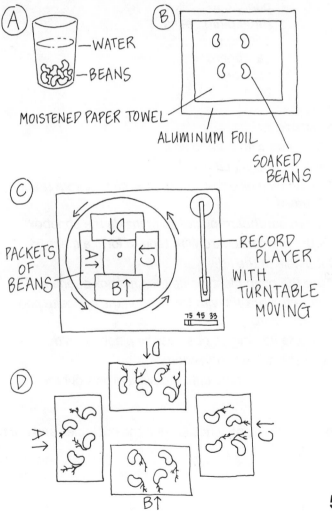

A) WATER
BEANS
MOISTENED PAPER TOWEL

B) ALUMINUM FOIL
SOAKED BEANS

C) PACKETS OF BEANS
RECORD PLAYER WITH TURNTABLE MOVING
75 45 33

D)

23. Flower Maze

Purpose To observe a plant winding its way toward light.

Materials *shoebox with a lid*
paper cup
three pinto beans
potting soil
cardboard
scissors
tape

Procedure
- *Fill the cup with potting soil.*
- *Plant the beans in the soil.*
- *Moisten the soil and allow the beans to sprout (about 5 to 7 days)*
- *Cut two cardboard pieces to fit inside the shoebox.*
- *Secure the cardboard with tape to form a maze.*
- *Cut a hole in the lid.*
- *Place the bean plant inside the shoebox at one end.*
- *Secure the box lid with the hole on the opposite end from the plant.*
- *Open the lid daily to observe the plants growth.*
- *Water the soil when needed.*
- *Continue to observe until the plant grows out the hole in the lid.*

Results The plant winds around the obstacles and out the hole in the lid.

Why? The plant is growing toward the light. This movement toward light is called *phototropism*. A build up of auxin, a plant growth chemical, occurs on the dark side of the stem. Auxin causes cells to grow longer on the dark side. This forces the stem to bend toward light.

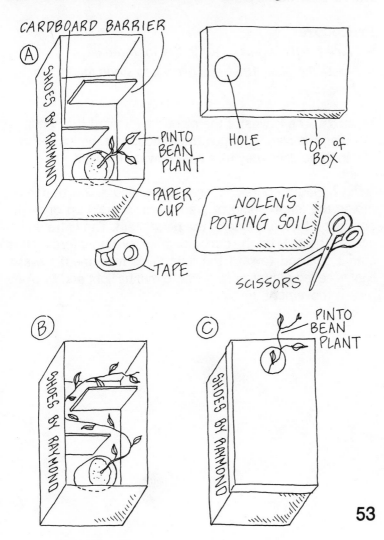

CARDBOARD BARRIER

Ⓐ

SHOES BY RAYMOND

PINTO BEAN PLANT

PAPER CUP

TAPE

HOLE

TOP of BOX

NOLEN'S POTTING SOIL

SCISSORS

Ⓑ

SHOES BY RAYMOND

Ⓒ

PINTO BEAN PLANT

SHOES BY RAYMOND

53

24. Light Seekers

Purpose To determine if plants do seek the light.

Materials *house plant*

Procedure

- *Place the plant next to a window for three days.*
- *Rotate the plant 180° and allow it to stand for another three days.*

Results The leaves of the plant turn toward the window. Rotating the plant changes the direction of the leaves, but within three days they turn back toward the light.

Why? Plants contain a chemical called auxin that promotes the lengthening of plant cells. A build up of auxin occurs on the dark side of the plant stem. The extra auxin causes the cells on the dark side to grow longer forcing the stems to bend toward the light. This movement toward light is called *phototropism*. Photo means light and tropism means movement.

55

25. Darkness Below

Purpose To demonstrate why green plant life does not occur below 100 meters in the ocean.

Materials *2 small green potted plants (same variety)*

Procedure
- *Place one of the plants in a sunny area, and the other plant in a dark closet or cabinet.*
- *Leave the plants for 7 days.*
- *Compare the color of the plants.*

Results The plant in the closet will be lighter in color and wilted.

Why? Plants need sunlight to undergo the energy making reaction called photosynthesis. Chlorophyll is a green pigment necessary in the photosynthesis reaction. Without the sunlight, the chlorophyll molecules are used up and not replenished causing the plant to look pale. In time, the plant will die without sunlight.

Green plants grow in the ocean to a depth of about 100 meters. They are more abundant near the surface and decrease with an increase in depth. The concentration of sunlight is greatest at the surface and totally disappears below 100 meters. Green plants cannot live below 100 meters.

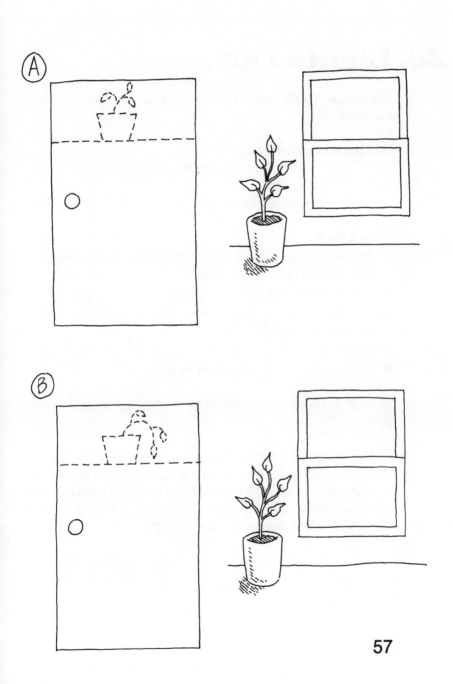

26. Lights Out

Purpose To determine the effect of sunlight on plant survival.

Materials *house plant*
black construction paper
scissors
tape (cellophane)

Procedure

■ *Cut two pieces of black construction paper large enough to cover one leaf on the plant.*
■ *Sandwich the leaf between the two paper pieces.*
■ *Tape the paper together. It is important that the leaf not receive any sunlight.*
■ *Wait 7 days.*
■ *Uncover the leaf and observe its color.*

Results The leaf is much paler than other leaves on the plant.

Why? A green chemical called chlorophyll gives leaves their green color. In the absence of sunlight, the green pigment is used up and not replenished in the leaf resulting in a light-colored leaf. Since chlorophyll is necessary for plant survival, the leaf will die without sunlight.

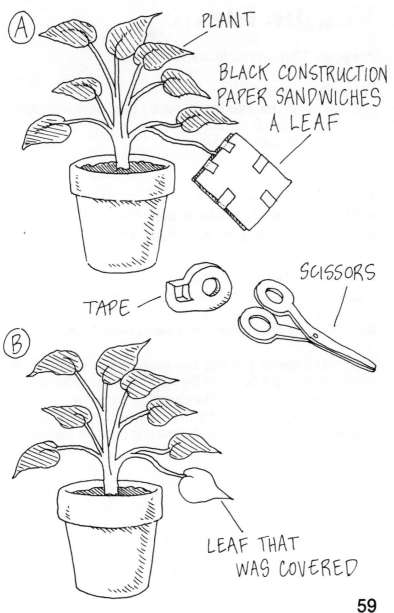

A PLANT

BLACK CONSTRUCTION
PAPER SANDWICHES
A LEAF

TAPE

SCISSORS

B

LEAF THAT
WAS COVERED

59

27. Veggie Plant

Purpose To grow plants from carrot tops.

Materials *sand*
carrot tops (ask an adult to cut the tops from several carrots)
shallow container

Procedure
- *Fill the container with sand.*
- *Thoroughly wet the sand with water.*
- *Insert the cut end of the carrot tops in the wet sand.*
- *Place in a lighted area.*
- *Keep the sand wet for 7 days.*
- *Observe the tops of the carrots for changes.*

Results Tiny green stems and leaves begin to grow.

Why? The carrot top has the base of the stem and a portion of the root on it. All the necessary parts for a productive plant are present. The carrot portion is the root and contains the food reserve for the plant. Supplying the plant with water allows the stem to grow and produce leaves.

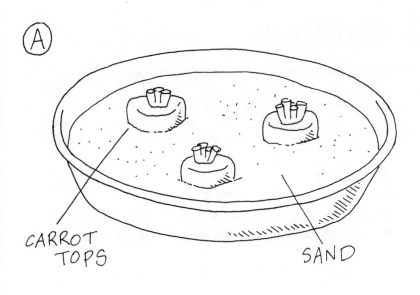

CARROT
TOPS

SAND

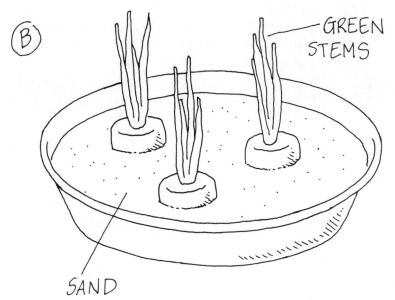

GREEN
STEMS

SAND

61

28. Cuttings

Purpose To grow a new plant from a cutting.

Materials *house plant, such as ivy*
scissors
jar

Procedure
- *Cut off a stem with leaves from the plant.*
- *Place the cut end of the stem in a jar filled with water.*
- *Observe the bottom of the stem for several days.*

Results Tiny roots start to grow on the stem.

Why? Many house plants and especially ivy will easily form roots on cut stems. This is one way in which plants produce new plants other than by seed growth. For the plant top to continue to grow, it must be planted in soil.

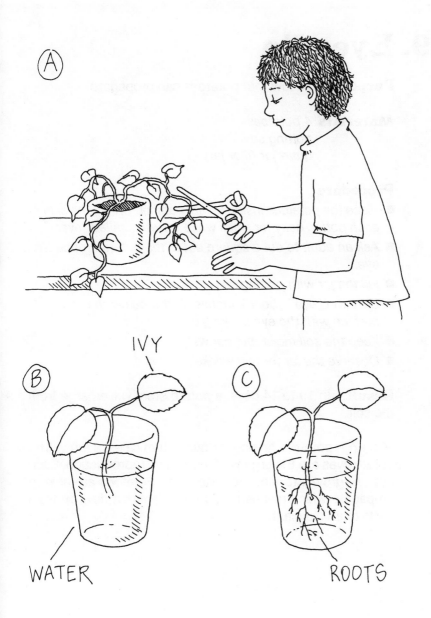

A

IVY

B

WATER

C

ROOTS

63

29. Eyes Up

Purpose To show that potatoes can propagate.

Materials *4 potatoes*
potting soil
quart jar (liter jar)

Procedure
- *Place the potatoes inside a dark cabinet. Check the skin of each potato daily for small white growths called "eyes."*
- *Ask an adult to cut a square out of the potato around the eye.*
- *Fill the jar with potting soil.*
- *Bury the "eye" about 2 inches (5 cm) below the soil's surface with the eye sticking up.*
- *Keep the soil moist, but not wet.*
- *Observe the jar for two weeks.*

Results In 10 to 14 days, a potato stem will emerge from the soil.

Why? A potato is an underground stem called a *tuber.* The potato eyes are the organs of vegetative reproduction. Each eye will grow into a new potato plant. Potatoes are able to propagate which means that a new plant can develop from parts of an old plant.

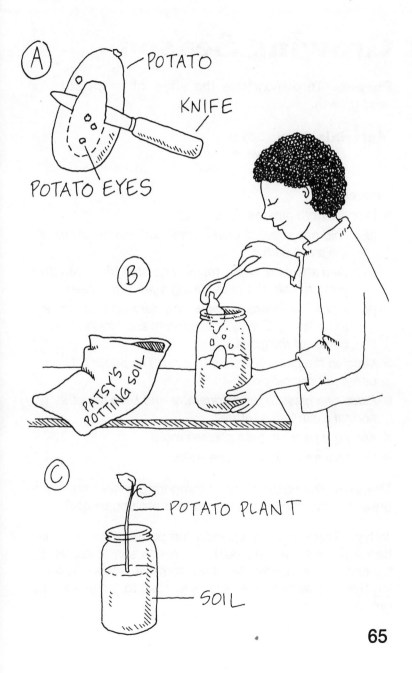

(A) POTATO
KNIFE
POTATO EYES

(B) PATSY'S POTTING SOIL

(C) POTATO PLANT
SOIL

65

30. Growing Season

Purpose To demonstrate the effect of temperature on seed growth.

Materials *8 pinto beans*
paper towels
2 drinking glasses

Procedure

■ *Prepare both glasses as follows:*
- *(a.) Fold one sheet of paper towel and line the inside of the glass with it.*
- *(b.) Wad sheets of paper towels and stuff them into the glass to hold the paper lining against the glass.*
- *(c.) Place four beans between the glass and the paper towel lining. Evenly space the beans around the center of the glass.*

■ *Moisten the paper towel with water. The paper is to be damp not dripping wet.*

■ *Place one glass in the refrigerator and keep the other at normal room temperature.*

■ *Keep the paper in both glasses moist.*

■ *Observe each glass for one week.*

Results The beans at room temperature have started to grow, but the ones in the refrigerator are unchanged.

Why? Seeds need a specific temperature to grow and beans require warmth. Very few seeds sprout during the fall and winter months. Most lay dormant, unchanging during the cold parts of the year, and start to grow when the ground warms.

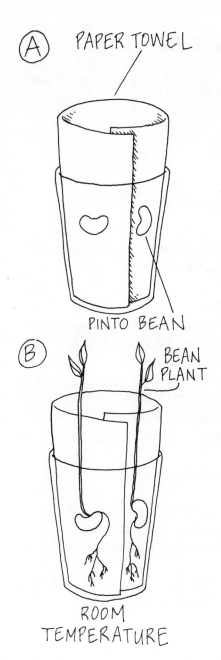

(A) PAPER TOWEL

PINTO BEAN

REFRIGERATOR

PAPER TOWEL

PINTO BEAN

(B) BEAN PLANT

ROOM TEMPERATURE

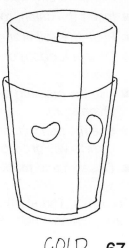

COLD

67

31. Growth Rate

Purpose To measure the growth rate of a plant stem grown in the shade.

Materials 2 green onions
glass
soil
ruler
marking pen, red or black

Procedure

■ Measure about 6 inches (15 cm) from the root of each onion and have an adult cut off the stem.

■ Fill the glass with soil.

■ Moisten the soil with water.

■ Stick the closed end of the marking pen into the soil near the glass and move it back and forth to make a hole. The hole needs to be large enough to bury the onion root 2 inches (5 cm) below the soil's surface.

■ Insert the onion, root down, into the hole.

■ Push the soil around the onion to secure it in place.

■ Do this for both onions. Place the glass away from a window.

■ Use the marking pen to color around the end of each onion stem.

■ Use the pen to mark the stems each day. The new growth will grow out of the outer skin covering.

■ Observe and mark the stems daily for 2 weeks.

Results The stems may grow at different rates, but they can grow as much as 12 inches (30 cm) in 2 weeks.

Why? Plants need water, nutrients, and sunlight to grow properly. Their growth changes when any one of these three factors is lacking. The lack of sufficient sunlight causes a plant to grow very tall. Many bedding plants have very long stems because they do not receive enough sunlight. Trees in a thick forest are often thin and very tall so that they can reach upward to the sun. Your onion plant has grown very tall because of the lack of sunlight.

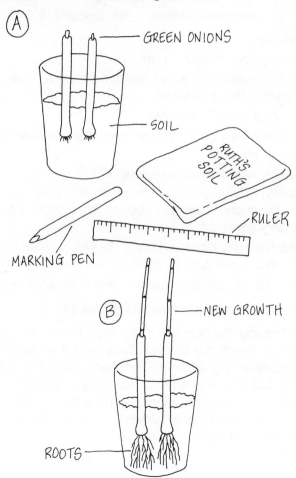

A — GREEN ONIONS

SOIL

RUTH'S POTTING SOIL

RULER

MARKING PEN

B — NEW GROWTH

ROOTS

32. Bon Appetit

Purpose To grow edible plant sprouts without soil.

Materials *paper towels*
glass
alpha or mung bean seeds
quart (liter) large mouth jar
measuring spoon —tablespoon (15 ml)

Procedure

- *Place 1 spoon of seeds in the jar.*
- *Cover the seeds with water and allow them to soak overnight in the refrigerator.*
- *Carefully drain off the water.*
- *Cover the jar with a wet paper towel that has been folded several times.*
- *Place the jar in a cool, dark cabinet.*
- *Each day, for 5 days, rinse the seeds with fresh warm water. Drain and cover with the wet towel. Return to the cool, dark cabinet.*
- *On the sixth day rinse and drain the seeds. Then place the jar in a sunny spot for three to four hours.*
- *Remove the sprouts from the jar, rinse thoroughly, and eat.*

Results The seeds grow into edible plants.

Why? Rinsing the sprouts daily kept them wet and allowed them to continue to grow. They were very pale before being placed in the sunlight. The sun turned the sprouts green. Growing plants without soil takes less space and their growth is not dependent on the weather. There are advantages to this type of growth, but only certain plants will grow without soil.

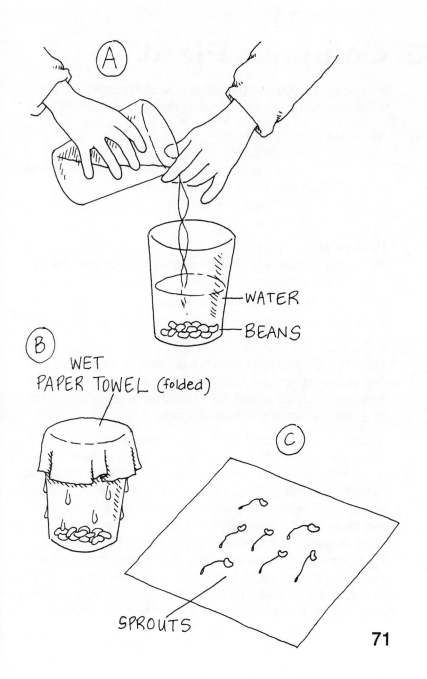

A

WATER

BEANS

B

WET
PAPER TOWEL (folded)

C

SPROUTS

71

33. Compass Plant

Purpose To observe the water-absorbing ability of lichens which may be used to explain the plants' north-seeking habit.

Materials *glass of water*
eye dropper
lichen samples (a pale green scaly or leaflike crust found on the bark of trees)
microscope or hand lens
compass

Procedure

- *Use the compass to determine the direction that the side of the tree with the most lichen growth is pointing.*
- *Observe your lichen samples under a microscope.*
- *Use the eye dropper to add drops of water on the lichen samples until they are wet.*

Results Close observation of the lichen reveals that it is not one plant, but a combination of two. One plant consists of very tiny colorless strands and the other is round and green. The lichen absorbs water like a sponge.

Why? The strands of colorless cells are parts of a fungus. Since the fungus has no chlorophyll, it cannot make its own food, but it does act like a sponge and absorbs water and holds it. The threads also attach to the bark of the tree and anchors the plant. The green algae manufactures sugar and starch which it shares with the fungus. The fact that the lichen is generally found on the north side of a tree has nothing to do with the magnetic field, but since moisture is a vital necessity for the plant it survives best where it can retain moisture the longest. The north and northeast sides of trees have the most shade and thus a lower evaporation rate.

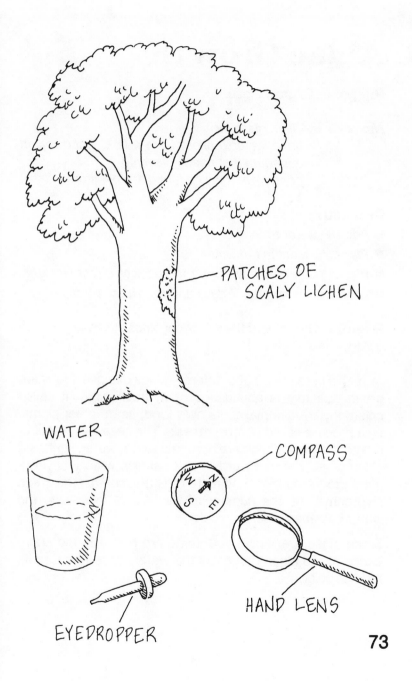

PATCHES OF
SCALY LICHEN

WATER

COMPASS

HAND LENS

EYEDROPPER

73

34. Algae Growth

Purpose To grow algae.

Materials *clear, glass jar*
pond water (collect from a lake, pond, or an aquarium that needs cleaning)
pond plant (may be found at a pet store or lake)

Procedure
- *Add the water to the jar.*
- *Place the plant in the water.*
- *Place the jar near a window that receives direct sunlight.*
- *Examine the jar after 7 days and then after 14 days.*

Results The color of the water becomes increasingly more green.

Why? There are 30,000 different kinds of algae. Many are green due to the abundance of a green pigment called chlorophyll. Algae makes its own food, as do other plants, by a process called photosynthesis. The necessary requirements for this reaction are carbon dioxide, water, light, and chlorophyll. The algae grows in its sunny, watery environment producing more and more cells that contain the green chlorophyll. As the number of these cells increases, the water becomes greener in color.

Some algae are brown and some are red. It is the abundance of red algae that gives the water in the Red Sea its reddish color.

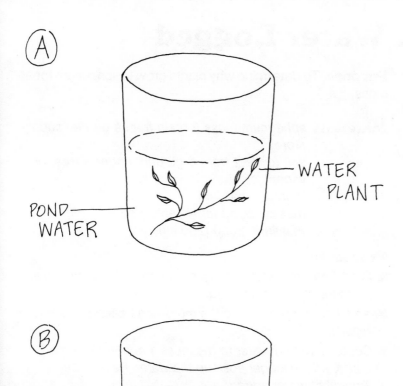

75

35. Water Logged

Purpose To determine why plants grow in sphagnum (peat moss).

Materials *sphagnum moss (obtain from a garden supply store)*
soil (collect from a garden, under a tree, or a vacant lot)
2 quart (liter) jars
measuring spoon—tablespoon (15 ml)
measuring cup (250 ml)

Procedure
- *Pour 1 cup of soil into one jar, and one cup of sphagnum moss into the remaining jar.*
- *Add 1 spoon of water to the moss and observe any results.*
- *Continue to add water to the moss 1 spoon at a time until it will no longer soak up the water. Record the amount of water added.*
- *Repeat the process by adding water 1 spoon at a time to the jar containing the soil.*
- *Record the amount of water that must be added before the soil no longer is able to soak it up.*
- *What would be the advantage of using sphagnum to grow plants in?*

Results The sphagnum moss is able to soak up much more water than the soil.

Why? Sphagnum moss is commonly called peat moss and is used in growing plants. The moss acts like a dry sponge

76

with cavities that the water can move into. Gardeners often mix the moss with soil or spread it around plants because the moss holds so much water. It also is used in potting plants that must be shipped to assure that they stay moist.

At one time, physicians used this moss to cover wounds because it absorbed liquids so well. It was observed that wounds bound with the moss became infected less often than those covered with other dressings.

PEAT MOSS   WATER   SOIL

II
Experiments in the Animal Kingdom

Introductory Zoology

Zoology is the study of animal life from simple one-celled organisms to multi-cellular organisms like mammals. How organisms live and how their bodies function is of the utmost interest to a zoologist—a person who studies animals. There are a great many kinds of organisms—more than 800,000 kinds of insects, about 9,000 kinds of birds, and snakes, spiders, mammals, fish. One person cannot know everything about *all* of these animals. Many scientists specialize and study one type of animal—an ichthyologist studies fish, an entomologist studies insects, and a bacteriologist studies bacteria. You will study a little about many different animals.

Upon completion of this section you will be able to determine the age of a fish, calculate the temperature from a cricket's chirping, explain how to raise earthworms and describe their reaction to light and other stimuli. Not only will you cultivate colorful mini-gardens of mold and fungi, but you will be able to identify a very special mold called penicillin. Your study of zoology will also include experiments to determine the effects of pollution on animal life.

Only a few of the many kinds of animals have been selected for study in this section. Hopefully, you will find them interesting enough to make you want to learn more about zoology.

36. Bread Mold

Purpose To grow a type of fungus called bread mold.

Materials *ziplock® bag*
bread slice
eye dropper

Procedure
- *Place the bread in the plastic bag.*
- *Put 10 drops of water inside the bag.*
- *Close the bag.*
- *Keep the bag in a dark, warm place for 3 to 5 days.*
- *Observe the bread through the plastic.*
- *Discard the bag and its contents after your observation.*

Results A black, hairy looking structure is growing on the bread.

Why? Mold is a form of fungus. It can grow and reproduce very quickly. Mold produces very tiny cells with hard coverings called *spores*. Spores are smaller than dust particles and float through the air. The slice of bread already has spores on it when placed in the plastic bag. The water, warmth, and darkness provide a good environment for the mold to grow.

Molds have good and bad uses. Some forms of mold make foods taste and smell bad, but there are foods that depend on mold for their good taste. Many cheeses are moldy and taste good. The greenish mold that forms on bread and oranges is used to make a medicine called penicillin.

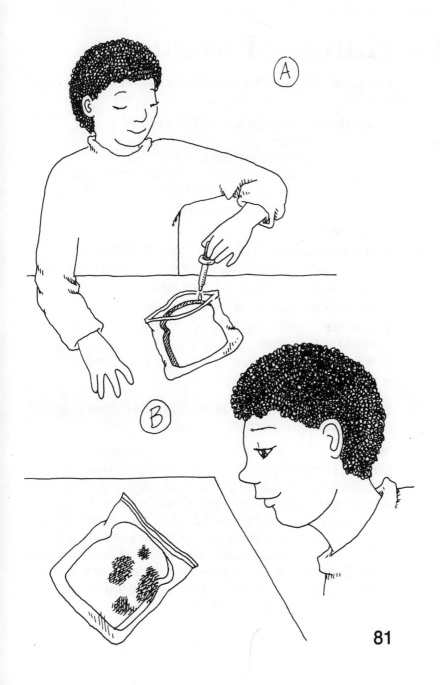

81

37. Hungry Fungus

Purpose To observe the effect that yeast has on a sugar solution.

Materials *1 package of powdered yeast*
sugar
glass soda bottle
measuring spoon —tablespoon (15 ml)
measuring cup (250 ml)
10-inch (25 cm) balloon

Procedure

- *Mix the package of yeast and 1 spoon of sugar in one cup of warm water. Be sure the water is warm, not hot.*
- *Pour the solution into the soda bottle.*
- *Add another cup of warm water to the bottle.*
- *Squeeze the air out of the balloon and place it over the mouth of the bottle.*
- *Place the bottle in a warm, dark place for 3 to 4 days.*
- *Observe the bottle daily.*

Results Bubbles are continuously being formed in the liquid. The balloon is partially inflated.

Why? Yeast is a fungus. It has no chlorophyll like other plants and cannot produce its own food. Like animals, yeast can use food such as sugar to produce energy. The yeast causes the sugar to change into alcohol, carbon dioxide gas, and energy. The bubbles observed in this experiment are carbon dioxide. This same gas causes bread to rise during baking as the bubbles push the moist dough up and outward. Gas holes can be seen in the finished bread. The nice smell from the baking of yeast bread is partially due to the evaporation of the alcohol produced.

82

(A)

DENNIS' SUGAR

Brenda's DRY YEAST

MEASURING SPOON

SODA

BALLOON

(B)

SODA

GAS BUBBLES

83

38. Bacterial Growth

Purpose To demonstrate the effect that temperature has on the growth of bacteria.

Materials *milk*
measuring cup (250 ml)
2 pint (500 ml) jars
refrigerator

Procedure
- *Put a cup of milk in each jar.*
- *Close each jar.*
- *Place one jar in the refrigerator.*
- *Place the second jar in a warm place.*
- *Examine the milk in each jar once a day for 7 days.*

Results The warm milk has thick, white lumps in it and smells sour. The cold milk looks and smells like drinkable milk.

Why? Warm temperatures promote the growth of bacteria that can cause food to spoil. Cooler temperatures slow down the bacteria growth, but milk will eventually spoil if left in the refrigerator long enough. The bacteria are present and grow very slowly when cold, but they do grow.

(A)

MILK

DANIEL'S
WHOLE
MILK

MILK

MILK

(B)

WARM MILK

COLD MILK

85

39. Mini-Organisms

Purpose To test the effect of preservatives on bacterial growth.

Materials *table salt*
white vinegar
3 small clear glasses
1 chicken bouillon cube
1 measuring cup (250 ml)
1 measuring spoon —teaspoon (5 ml)
masking tape
marking pen

Procedure
- *Dissolve the bouillon cube in one cup (250 ml) of hot water from the faucet.*
- *Equally divide the solution between the three glasses.*
- *Add 1 spoon of salt to one of the glasses and label the glass salt as in the diagram; make the label with the masking tape.*
- *Add 1 spoon of vinegar to the second glass and label it vinegar.*
- *The last glass is to be labeled control because it will not contain a preservative.*
- *Place the three glasses in a warm place for 2 days. Which glass is cloudier?*

Results The solution containing vinegar is clearer than the others. The control is the most cloudy.

86

Why? The cloudiness is due to the presence of large quantities of bacteria. The glasses containing preservatives are clearer than the control because the preservatives inhibit, slow down, the growth of bacteria. Vinegar seems to have inhibited the bacterial growth the best.

DAVIN'S SALT

WADE'S VINEGAR

SALT

VINEGAR

CONTROL

MODERATELY CLOUDY

CLEAR

VERY CLOUDY

CHICKEN BULLION CUBES

MEASURING SPOON

MASKING TAPE

MEASURING CUP

40. Coconut Cultures

Purpose To determine where molds grow best.

Materials *coconut*
rubberband
bread sack

Procedure

- *Ask an adult to break the coconut and pour out the liquid.*
- *Expose the open coconut to the air for 2 hours.*
- *Put the coconut pieces back together and secure with a rubberband.*
- *Place the coconut in a bread sack and place in a warm dark place for one week.*
- *Look at the outside and inside of the coconut daily for any growths.*

Results The outside of the coconut seems unchanged while the inside has different colored spots on it.

Why? Mold is a form of fungus, a Latin word meaning food-robbing. The colored coconut garden contains different types of fungi that came from the air. They can not make their own food because they have no chlorophyll so they must steal food from their host organism. Fungi are all around you—in the air, on your clothes, skin, hair—everywhere. They must have air, food, and water to live and when they land on a nice moist airy piece of food like your coconut, they thrive very well.

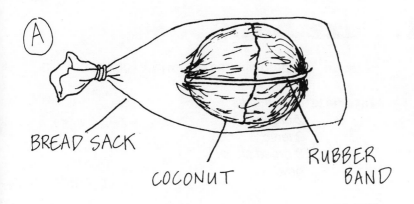

Ⓐ

BREAD SACK

COCONUT

RUBBER
BAND

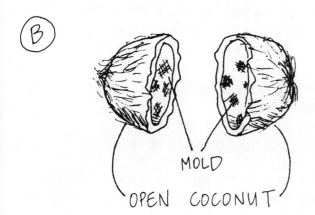

Ⓑ

MOLD

OPEN COCONUT

89

41. Fuzz Balls

Purpose To determine the best way to grow penicillin.

Materials *cotton balls*
2 oranges
2 lemons
2 bread sacks
bowl

Procedure
- *Rub the fruit on the floor.*
- *Place the fruit in a bowl exposed to the air for one day.*
- *Place in each bread sack an orange, a lemon, and a cotton ball wet with water.*
- *Secure the ends of the sacks.*
- *Place one sack in the refrigerator and the other in a warm dark place.*
- *Leave the sacks closed for two weeks.*
- *Observe the fruit through the sacks daily.*

Results The fruit in the refrigerator looks the same or possibly a bit dryer, but the other fruit has turned into blue-green fuzzy balls.

Why? The green powdery growth on the outside of the fruit is penicillius. Under a microscope this mold looks like a small brush thus it was named from the Latin word penicillus meaning a paint brush. Because brushes were used to write with at one time, our modern writing tool, the pencil, is named after the Latin word for paintbrush. Molds can grow in hot places, but they grow faster and in more abundance in moist warm places. This is why foods become more moldy in the summertime. Placing bread in a bread box or on top of a refrigerator causes them to mold more quickly. Cooling foods slows down the growth of mold and freezing keeps foods fresh for much longer periods of time.

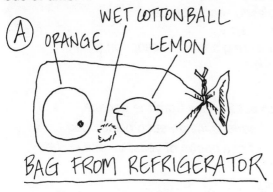

(A) ORANGE   WET COTTON BALL   LEMON

BAG FROM REFRIGERATOR

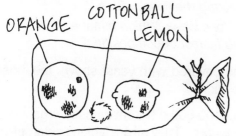

ORANGE   COTTON BALL   LEMON

BAG LEFT OUT OF REFRIGERATOR

(B)   ← MAGNIFIED

PAINT BRUSH MOLD

42. Decomposers

Purpose To observe the effects of yeast on food decomposition.

Materials *banana*
2 plastic sandwich bags
dry yeast
measuring spoon —teaspoon (5 ml)
marker

Procedure

- *Ask an adult to cut 2 slices from the banana.*
- *Place a slice of banana inside each plastic bag.*
- *Sprinkle one-half of a spoon of yeast on one of the banana slices.*
- *Close both bags.*
- *Mark the bag containing the yeast with a Y.*
- *Check each bag for one week. Which banana slice shows the most and fastest decomposition?*

Results The banana covered with yeast shows the most and fastest decomposition.

Why? Yeast is one of 100,000 different kinds of organisms that make up the fungi group. They all are lacking chlorophyll and must depend on other organisms for food. The yeast feeds on the banana causing it to break into smaller parts. This breakdown is referred to as *decay.* Decomposers are an important part of our world because there is much dead material that must be broken into· smaller parts and reused by plants and animals. The fertilizer used on plants and gardens has many decomposers working in it to make the material usable by the plants.

(A) PLASTIC SANDWICH BAGS

BANANA SLICE WITH YEAST

PLAIN BANANA SLICE

LARRY'S ACTIVE YEAST

MEASURING SPOON

BANANA

(B) AFTER ONE WEEK:

BANANA SLICE WITH YEAST

PLAIN BANANA SLICE

93

43. Fireflies

Purpose To determine if the light from fireflies gives off heat.

Materials *fireflies*
2 glass jars with lids
2 thermometers (must fit inside the jars)

Procedure
- *On a night when fireflies are plentiful catch as many as you can and place them in a jar. It is easiest to catch them with your hands after they land on a surface.*
- *Put a thermometer into the jar with the fireflies and another thermometer in the empty jar.*
- *Record the temperature of each jar after 30 minutes.*
- *Does the temperature differ in the jars?*

Results Depending on the number of fireflies in the jar, the temperature may be slightly higher in the jar with the insects.

Why? The luminescence, or cold light, produced by the fireflies gives off no heat. Any possible rise in temperature in the jar is just due to body heat given off by the insects. Light produced by living organisms is called *bioluminescence*. The light is caused by the chemical luciferin. When this chemical combines with oxygen it gives off light. The color intensity and length of time between flashes depends on the species. See Experiment 44 *Flashers* for more information about the light from fireflies.

94

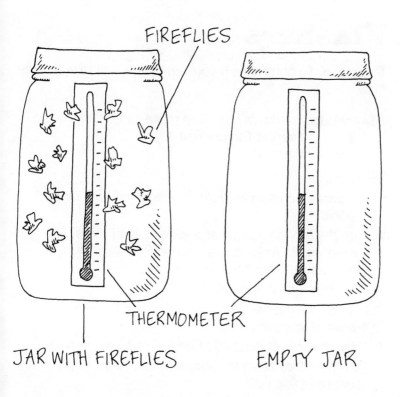

FIREFLIES

THERMOMETER

JAR WITH FIREFLIES

EMPTY JAR

44. Flashers

Purpose To determine if you can communicate with fireflies.

Materials *fireflies in a jar (use those caught for the Fireflies Experiment 43)*
flashlight

Procedure
- *In a darkened room hold the flashlight near the jar of fireflies.*
- *Turn the light on and off at one-second intervals. The easiest way to judge a one-second interval is to say these words "One thousand and one."*
- *Flash the light at least 10 times.*
- *Change the intervals to 2 seconds, then 3 and finally 4-second intervals.*
- *Flash the light at least 10 times for each time interval.*
- *Do the fireflies seem to respond to any of the time intervals of flashes?*

Results The fireflies seem to respond to the light flashes. It will depend on the species as to the interval of flashes that they will most likely respond to.

Why? Fireflies are beetles that have a layer of light-producing cells on their abdomen. These cells contain luciferin, a chemical that gives off light when combined with oxygen. The female has no wings and can be found on the ground. Her light is much brighter. It is believed that the rhythm of flashes is done to attract a mate. They usually flash their light in time intervals ranging from 1 to 4 seconds depending on the species.

FIREFLIES

FLASHLIGHT

45. Distinctive

Purpose To determine how butterflies and moths differ.

Materials *coat hanger*
pillowcase
2 large jars
stocking
2 rubberbands
broom handle or long stick
butterfly and moth (instructions for catching below)

Procedure

■ *Make an insect net by bending a coat hanger into a hoop. Attach the pillowcase to the hoop and secure the ends of the hoop to the broom handle. (This can be done by twisting the ends of the wire around the handle.)*

■ *Use the insect net to catch a butterfly and a moth for this study.*

■ *Place the captured insects in separate jars. You can remove them from the pillowcase net by holding the net over the jar and gently shaking out the insect.*

■ *Cover both jars with a piece of stocking and secure with a rubberband.*

■ *View both insects through the glass and record their similarities and differences.*

■ *Do they hold their wings the same? How about the shape of their antennae, are they the same? Is there any difference in the size of their abdomen? You can discover the answers to these questions and record more differences between these two insects simply by visual observation.*

98

Results Butterflies and moths are alike in the number of legs, wings, and antennae they have. They are different in the way that the wings are held, the shape of the antennae, and the abdomen. Other differences and similarities are not visually obvious.

Why? Both butterflies and moths have three pairs of jointed legs, two pairs of wings that are covered with tiny scales which produce their brilliant colors and patterns. One should try not to touch their wings because even light pressures can remove scales and seriously injure the insect. Though butterflies and moths resemble they still have very distinctive characteristics. The butterfly holds its wings upward when resting and the moth rests with its wings spread out. Both insects have slender, jointed, movable appendages on their heads called *antennae*. The butterfly's antennae is slender and clubbed at the end. Moth's have all shapes and sizes, but they are never clubbed and many are feathery. The body and abdomen, of the moth is thicker and larger than the slender shaped butterfly. For more information about these insects, use a reference guide.

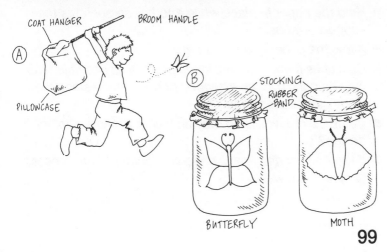

COAT HANGER   BROOM HANDLE

(A)

PILLOWCASE

(B)

STOCKING

RUBBER BAND

BUTTERFLY   MOTH

46. Geometric Designs

Purpose To determine if spider webs have the same geometric design.

Materials *enamel spray paint (any bright color)*
hairspray
scissors
white construction paper

Procedure

- *The best time to find spider webs is in the early morning of a spring or summer day.*
- *Pick out several webs suitable for collecting and wait a few hours for the dew to dry.* Caution: *be sure the spider is gone before continuing.*
- *Spray the web with enamel spray paint.*
- *Immediately spray a piece of white construction paper with hairspray, and push the tacky paper against the wet web.*
- *Hold the paper in place while another person cuts the support strands.*
- *Allow the paper and web to dry.*
- *Collect as many different kinds of webs as possible. This may be done over an extended period of time since the webs can be preserved.*
- *Compare the webs. Do they all have the same geometric design?*
- *If the opportunity arises observe a spider in the process of spinning a web.*

100

Results Spiders of the same species do build the same geometrically designed web, but the design changes from one species to another.

Why? The building of the web is not a learned ability. It is an inborn trait which means the baby spider has within its brain the plan of its future webs.

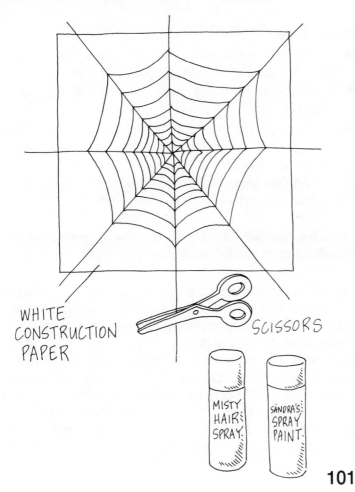

WHITE
CONSTRUCTION
PAPER

SCISSORS

MISTY HAIR SPRAY

SANDRA'S SPRAY PAINT

47. Telegraph Lines

Purpose To determine how a spider evaluates the size of an intruder.

Materials *string*
 a partner

Procedure

- *Stretch the string between two stationary objects. A door knob and a table leg are good choices.*
- *At one end of the string, gently place the tips of your fingers on top of the string.*
- *Have your partner to pluck the opposite end of the string while you look away. You do not want to see how firmly the string is being plucked.*
- *Your partner should pluck the string with varying degrees of firmness: gently to very firm.*

Results You will be able to feel the varying degrees of vibrations of the string with your finger tips.

Why? When the string is plucked at one end, it causes the entire string to vibrate. A gentle touch produces a weak vibration, and a more aggressive plucking causes the entire string to vibrate briskly. Spiders feel the vibration of their web. The web acts like a telegraph line. When the web shakes, the spider senses the movement because it has sensory hairs on its legs. If the vibration is very weak, the spider ignores it. Very large vibrations could mean a prey that would injure the spider so it often hides or cuts the strand. A medium vibration lets the spider know that the intruder is small enough to catch for dinner and it rushes toward the source of vibration to invite the visitor to stay awhile. The spider quickly wraps the trapped visitor in strands of silk before it can escape from the sticky web.

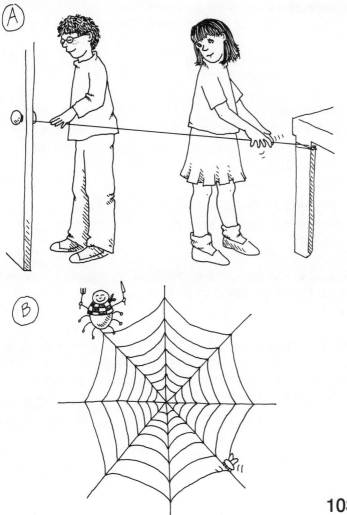

48. Cricket Thermometer

Purpose To determine the temperature from a cricket's chirp.

Materials *watch with a second hand*
cricket (may be purchased from a live bait store)
jar
nylon stocking
rubberband

Procedure
- *Catch a cricket and place it in the jar. Stretch the stocking over the mouth of the jar and secure with the rubberband.*
- *Count the cricket chirps in 15 seconds.*
- *Add forty to the number of chirps counted.*
- *Repeat this process several times before releasing the cricket.*

Results The sum of the chirps in 15 seconds plus forty equals the air temperature in degrees Fahrenheit around the cricket.

Why? The temperature affects the activity of many animals. Cold weather can make them sluggish while warmer weather increases their activity. Crickets chirp more in warm weather and less when it is cold.

STOCKING

RUBBER BAND

CRICKET

49. Grasshopper

Purpose To study the parts of a grasshopper.

Materials *insect net (instructions found in* Experiment 45
Distinctive)
grasshopper (instruction for catching below)
magnifying glass
plastic bag

Procedure

- *Use the insect net to catch a grasshopper. It would be easier if you find a dead grasshopper for this study, but if a dead grasshopper is not found catch a live one with the net and place it in a plastic bag.*
- *Move the live grasshopper to the end of the bag so that it cannot move around.*
- *Use the magnifying glass to study the insect.*
- *Find the three main parts of the grasshopper. Also find the other parts that are labeled.*

Results The three divisions of the body that are easily seen are the legs and wings. With the aid of the magnifying glass, the other body parts are visible.

Why? Grasshoppers like all insects have three main body parts, the head, thorax, and abdomen; three pairs of legs; two pairs of wings; two antennae; a mouth; and compound and simple eyes.

Try This Do a little research and find out what each body does. Study other insects, like a cricket, to see if they contain the same body parts.

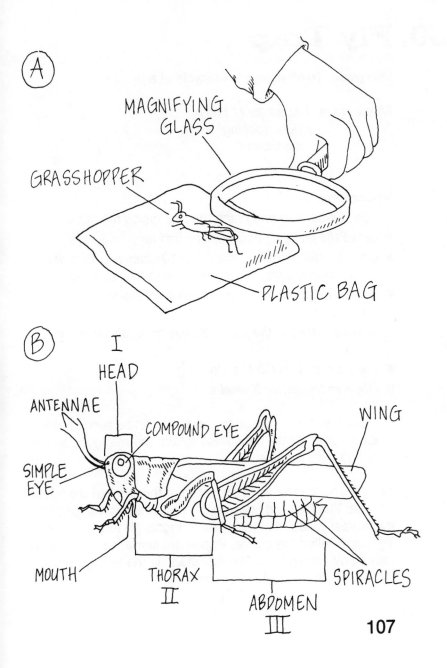

A

MAGNIFYING
GLASS

GRASSHOPPER

PLASTIC BAG

B

I
HEAD

ANTENNAE

COMPOUND EYE

WING

SIMPLE
EYE

MOUTH

THORAX
II

ABDOMEN
III

SPIRACLES

107

50. Fly Trap

Purpose To observe the lifecycle of a fly.

Materials *1 quart jar (1 liter)*
nylon stocking
rubberband
banana

Procedure

- *Peel the banana and place the fruit inside the open jar.*
- *Leave the jar open and undisturbed for 3 to 5 days.*
- *Observe the jar daily. When 5 to 10 small fruit flies are seen inside the jar, cover the top with the stocking.*
- *Secure the stocking over the mouth of the jar with a rubberband.*
- *Leave the flies in the jar for 3 days then release all of them.*
- *Recover the jar with the stocking.*
- *Observe the jar for 2 weeks.*

Results Within a few days, maggots can be seen crawling around. Later, small capsules replace the maggots and finally new flies emerge.

Why? The fruit flies are attracted to the smell of the ripening fruit. The flies laid eggs on the fruit which developed into the larvae, called maggots. The maggots go through a resting stage called the pupae. Pupae are similar to the cocoon formed by caterpillars. The last stage is the emerging adult fly and the cycle starts over again.

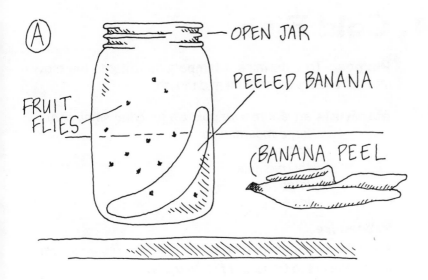

A — OPEN JAR

FRUIT FLIES

PEELED BANANA

BANANA PEEL

B

STOCKING

RUBBER BAND

MAGGOTS

109

51. Cold Fish

Purpose To determine if temperature affects the movement of a fish's operculum and mouth.

Materials *aquarium with goldfish (or other small fish)*
large-mouthed jar
fish net
thermometer
large bowl
ice

Procedure

- *Fill the large-mouthed jar with water from the aquarium.*
- *Use the net to transfer a fish to the jar.*
- *Allow the fish 30 minutes to adjust to its new environment.*
- *Count and record the number of times the fish opens and closes its mouth and operculum.*
- *Place the jar in the bowl.*
- *Fill the bowl one-half full with ice and then add enough water to fill the bowl. Do not add anything to the jar containing the fish.*
- *Wait until the temperature in the jar reads 10 degrees Celsius and again count the number of times the fish opens and closes its mouth and operculum in one minute.*

Results There is more movement when the water temperature was warmer.

Why? Animals conserve energy when in a cold environment. Their body loses heat thus losing energy when the temperature around them is cold. The body movements slow down to conserve energy.

110

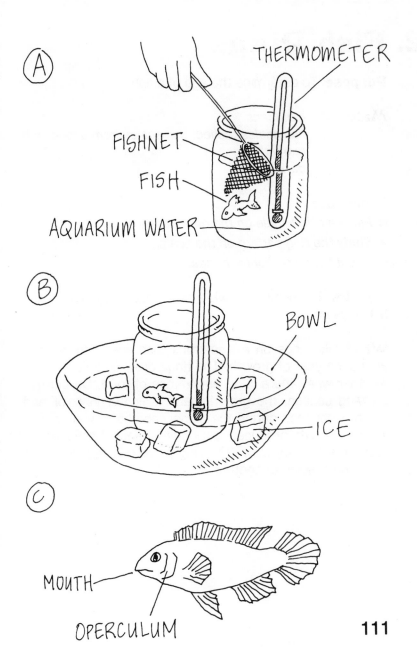

A

THERMOMETER

FISHNET

FISH

AQUARIUM WATER

B

BOWL

ICE

C

MOUTH

OPERCULUM

111

52. Fish Rings

Purpose To determine the age of a fish.

Materials *hand lens*
fish scales (collect fish scales from a local fish market)
dark paper

Procedure
- *Place a dried scale on the dark paper.*
- *Study the ring pattern on the scale.*
- *Count the wide, lighter bands.*

Results The number of wide bands equals the age of the fish in years.

Why? Like rings on a tree trunk, fish scales form rings with each year of growth. The rings grow fastest in warm weather when there is an abundance of food. During this growing season, the growth band is lighter in color and much wider than during the colder months of winter. The winter growth produces dark slim bands because the growth is so very slow. The ring pattern varies in design from one species to another.

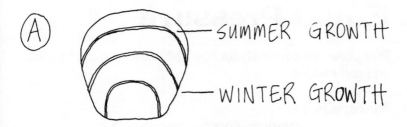

(A) — SUMMER GROWTH
— WINTER GROWTH

(B)

FISH SCALES

HAND LENS

DARK PAPER

53. Equal Pressure

Purpose To demonstrate how fish cells respond to fresh and salty water.

Materials *salt*
measuring spoon —teaspoon (5 ml)
2 shallow bowls
1 small cucumber
masking tape
marker

Procedure
- *Fill both bowls one-half full with water.*
- *Stir 1 spoon of salt into one of the bowls, label this bowl salt using the tape to make the label.*
- *Have an adult cut the cucumber into thin circular slices.*
- *Place 3 slices of cucumber into each bowl.*
- *Wait 30 minutes.*
- *Remove the slices and test their flexibility by carefully using your fingers to bend them back and forth.*
- *Now switch the slices, placing the ones that were previously in the salt water into the pure water, and the pure water slices go into the salty water.*
- *Wait 30 minutes and again test the flexibility.*

Results The cucumber slices are limp after soaking in the salt water and firmer in the pure water.

Why? Water moves into and out of living cells through the cell membrane. This movement is called *osmosis*. The water moves across the membrane toward where there are more dissolved materials in the water. Water moves out of the cells into the surrounding salty water because there are more salt particles in the water in the bowl than there is inside the cell. Removal of water is called *dehydration.* Fish in salt water tend to dehydrate and they compensate for this water loss from their cells by drinking large amounts of sea water. They excrete salt from their gills and their kidneys remove very little water from the body. Freshwater fish, however, would bloat because the opposite happens to them. Water is absorbed *into* their cells. The surrounding medium is *less* salty. Therefore, they excrete large amounts of water through their kidneys. Both types of fish have to compensate for the loss and gain of water by their cells due to their environment.

54. Holding On

Purpose To demonstrate how some sea organisms, such as sea anemones, secure themselves to rocks.

Materials *suction cup (the type used to secure hanging crafts to windows works well)*
rock

Procedure
- *Wet the suction cup and press it against the rock.*
- *Pick the rock up by holding onto the suction cup.*

Results The suction cup sticks so securely that the rock can be lifted.

Why? Pressing the cup against the rock forces the air out of the cup. The water forms a seal around the outside preventing the air from re-entering the cup. The air in the room actually pushes with so much force on the outside of the cup that it is held tightly against the rock. The suction cups on sea anemones work the same way. Under the water, the suction cups on the organisms are held tightly against rocks by the pressure of the water.

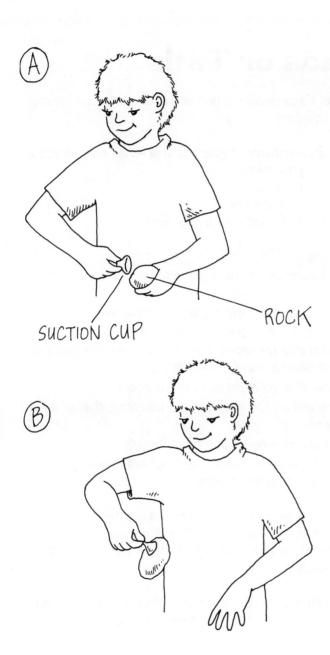

SUCTION CUP

ROCK

117

55. Heads or Tails

Purpose To determine if one end of an earthworm is more sensitive to odors.

Materials *earthworms (purchase at a bait shop or dig up*
  your own)
  paper towel
  cotton balls
  fingernail polish remover

Procedure
- *Place several worms on a paper towel moistened with water.*
- *Wet the cotton ball with fingernail polish remover.*
- *Hold the wet cotton ball near, but not touching the front or head end of the worm. This will be the end closest to the wide band around the worm's body.*
- *How does the worm respond to the odor?*
- *Hold the wet cotton near, but not touching, the tail end of the worm.*
- *Is there any difference in the response?*
- *Try holding the wet cotton near, but not touching other sections of the worm's body.*

Results The worm shows no area of greater sensitivity to the odor on the cotton ball. The worm makes an effort to move away from the irritating smell no matter where the cotton is placed.

Why? Earthworms do not have obvious sense organs, such as a nose, but they do have a nervous system that

118

responds to stimuli such as odors. They have a brain at the front end of the body with a large nerve cord extending all the way to the tail. Each body segment also has a mass of nerve tissue that controls activities within the segment. This is why the worm responds to odor at any place on its body.

119

56. Earthworm Farm

Purpose To produce an environment suitable for earth-worms.

Materials *1 quart (liter) jar*
2 cups (500 ml) of soil
1 cup (250 ml) humus (partially decayed leaves and roots)
earthworms (from a bait shop or dig your own)
apple peelings
dark construction paper
rubberband

Procedure
- *Pour the soil into the jar.*
- *Moisten the soil with the water.*
- *Sprinkle the humus over the soil.*
- *Put the worms into the jar.*
- *Add the apple peelings.*
- *Wrap the paper around the jar and secure with a rubberband. Place the jar in a cool place.*
- *Remove the paper and observe the jar every day for one week.*

Results The worms start wiggling and burrow into the soil. Tunnels are seen in the soil after a few days. The apple peelings disappear and casts appear on the surface of the soil.

Why? Earthworms are very beneficial because they loosen and enrich the soil. On the average, there are 50,000 worms per acre of soil and they eat about 18 wagonloads of soil every year. They do not have a jaw or teeth, but a muscle draws soil particles into their mouth. The worm extracts food from the soil and the remaining part of the soil passes through the worm's body unchanged. Casts containing the undigested soil are deposited on the surface of the soil.

It is important to keep the soil moist because it is through their moist skin that earthworms absorb the oxygen found in the air spaces throughout the soil.

57. Floaters

Purpose To determine why earthworms surface during a heavy rain.

Materials *container of earthworms and soil (can be purchased at a bait shop)*
one-half cup (125 ml) of aquarium gravel (purchase at a pet store)

Procedure
- *Pour water into the cup containing the gravel until the water covers the gravel.*
- *Explain why there are bubbles in the water. Why do they quit forming?*
- *Pour water into the container of earthworms and soil until the soil is covered.*
- *Did bubbles rise from the soil? How did the earthworms respond to the water?*

Results Bubbles rise for a short time when water is added to gravel or soil. The earthworms rose to the top of the wet soil.

Why? The water pushed the air out of the cavities in the gravel and since there are air spaces in the soil the air was replaced by the water in the soil. The bubbles seen were air bubbles and they stopped when all of the air was displaced by the water. The worms surfaced because of the lack of or low level of oxygen in the soil. During heavy rains, worms are often seen on the surface of soil and they are seeking oxygen.

122

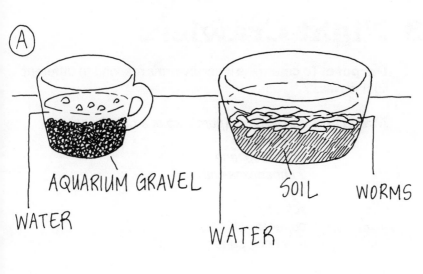

(A)

WATER

AQUARIUM GRAVEL

SOIL   WORMS

WATER

(B)

EARTHWORM

NERVE CORD

BRAIN

123

58. Night Crawlers

Purpose To determine if earthworms respond to different light waves.

Materials *earthworms (purchase at a bait shop)*
2 flashlights
red cellophane
2 shoeboxes with lids
tape
scissors
paper towels
notebook paper

Procedure

- *Prepare both shoeboxes by putting a circular hole in one end of each lid. The hole should be smaller than the flashlight's end.*
- *Tape notebook paper to the lids of each box so that it hangs about one inch (2 1/2 cm) from the floor of the shoeboxes, and about four inches (10 cm) from the end opposite the hole in the lid (see diagram).*
- *Place moistened paper towels in the bottom of each box.*
- *Position five earthworms in each box under where the hole in the lid will be.*
- *Place a flashlight over one of the holes, and turn it on.*
- *Cover the second hole with four layers of red cellophane. Position the flashlight over the hole and turn it on.*
- *Leave both boxes undisturbed for 30 minutes.*
- *Remove the flashlights and open the lids.*
- *Observe the position of the worms.*

Results The worms have crawled away from the white light and are under the paper partition where it is darker. The worms under the red light have made little or no change in their position.

Why? Earthworms have a nervous system with a simple brain. There are no obvious sense organs such as eyes or ears, but the worms respond to stimuli such as white light. The worms do not respond to red lightwaves. This fact helps fishermen when searching for worms at night. Earthworms often surface at night and, therefore, are referred to as night crawlers.

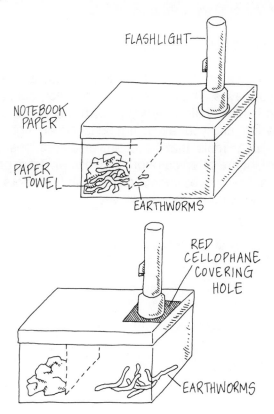

FLASHLIGHT

NOTEBOOK PAPER

PAPER TOWEL

EARTHWORMS

RED CELLOPHANE COVERING HOLE

EARTHWORMS

59. Hidden Picture

Purpose To observe the camouflaging technique of animals.

Materials *red, transparent, plastic folder*
pale yellow crayon
white typing paper

Procedure

■ *Draw a bird on the white paper with the yellow crayon.*

■ *Cover the drawing with the red folder.*

Results The yellow bird disappears.

Why? The yellow bird and red folder both are reflecting light to your eyes. The red is not a pure color, but has some yellow in it. This yellow blends in with the yellow from the bird drawing, and your eye is not sensitive enough to separate them. Animals that have similar colorations as their environment are often camouflaged, hidden, from prey. The stalking animal's eyes cannot distinguish the colors enough to separate its meal from the leaves.

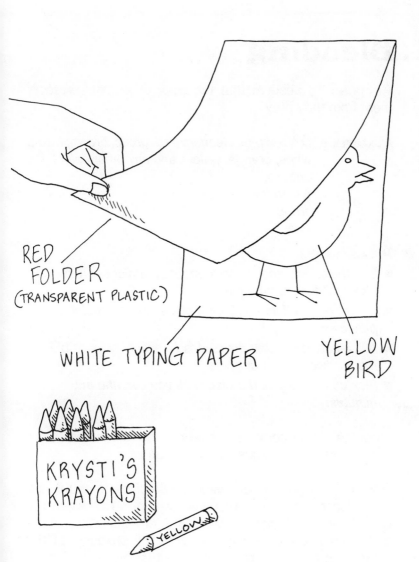

RED
FOLDER
(TRANSPARENT PLASTIC)

WHITE TYPING PAPER

YELLOW
BIRD

KRYSTI'S
KRAYONS

YELLOW

127

60. Blending

Purpose To observe that the color of animals protects them from their prey.

Materials *colored pipe cleaners (red, green, brown, black, white, orange, yellow, and any other colors you choose)*
4 wooden stakes
string
ruler

Procedure

- *Use the stakes and string to mark off a plot of grass about 20-foot (6 m) square.*
- *Cut 20 one-half inch (13 mm) pieces of each color of pipe cleaner.*
- *Ask a partner to sow the pieces as evenly as possible in the marked off plot of grass.*
- *Pick up as many of the pieces as you can find in 5 minutes.*

Results Some colors are easily found and others more difficult. All of the pieces were not found.

Why? If the grass is the same shade of green as the colored pieces then it is difficult to distinguish between the two. Colors that look alike were harder to find. Some of the darker colored pieces blend in with the shadows of the grass. It is the same color blending that protects animals from their prey. A white bunny is hard to see when sitting on a field of snow, and green snakes blend in very well on a lawn of green grass.

128

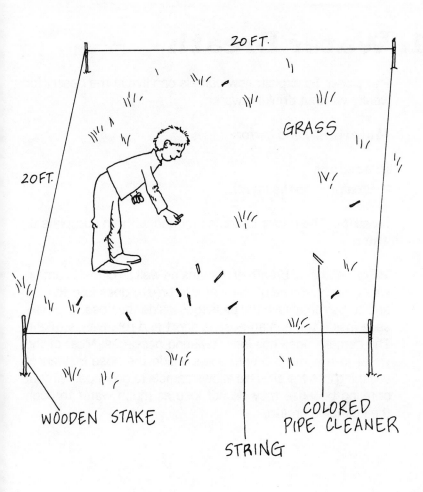

20 FT.

20 FT.

GRASS

WOODEN STAKE

STRING

COLORED
PIPE CLEANER

129

61. Water Breath

Purpose To explain how camels can live in the desert for weeks without drinking water.

Materials *hand mirror*

Procedure
■ *Breathe onto the mirror*

Results The mirror becomes fogged with tiny droplets of water.

Why? Exhaled breath of humans as well as camels contain water vapor. Some of the water in breath goes into the air, and some remains in the passages inside the nose. The passage inside the human nose is short and relatively straight. The camel's nose has long, twisting passages. Most of the water in a camel's breath stays inside the nose instead of escaping into the air. This allows camels to go longer without drinking because they do not lose as much water through their exhaled breath.

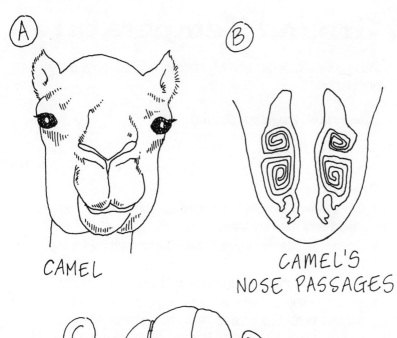

A

CAMEL

B

CAMEL'S
NOSE PASSAGES

C

62. Ground Temperature

Purpose To determine why desert animals spend their day underground.

Materials *2 outdoor thermometers*
trowel
white towel

Procedure
- *Dig a hole 4 inches (10 cm) deep and large enough to insert one thermometer.*
- *Cover the hole containing the thermometer with the towel.*
- *Lay the second thermometer on top of the ground.*
- *Wait 5 minutes then read the temperature on each thermometer. Be sure to read the underground thermometer as soon as it is removed from the ground.*

Results The temperature in the hole is lower than that on top of the ground.

Why? The sun's rays heat the air and all materials that they touch including the liquid in the thermometer. The soil on top of the ground gets much hotter because of the direct sun's rays. The soil in the hole stays cooler because no direct heat is applied. Desert animals dig holes into the ground and stay there during the heat of the day to stay cool.

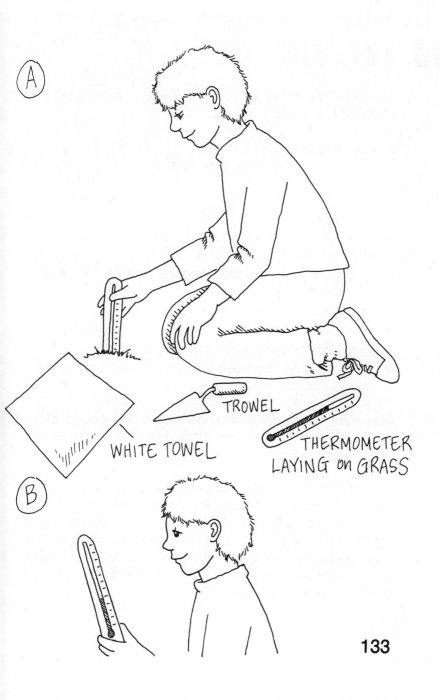

A

TROWEL

WHITE TOWEL

THERMOMETER
LAYING on GRASS

B

133

63. Lift Off

Purpose To determine why the shape of a bird's wing is important for flight.

Materials *scissors*
1 sheet of notebook paper
ruler

Procedure

- *Cut a one inch (2 1/2 cm) strip across the sheet of notebook paper.*
- *Hold one end of the paper against your chin, just below your bottom lip (see diagram).*
- *Blow across the top of the paper.*
- *Where was the air moving fastest, on top or below the paper? How did this affect the paper?*
- *How would the shape of a bird's wing have to affect the speed of air moving across it?*

Results The air was flowing quickly above the paper strip. The paper lifted toward the stream of air as long as you continued to blow.

Why? The faster the air moves, the less pressure it exerts on objects above and below it. The air below the paper is still pushing equally in all directions, thus the upward push on the paper is greater than the downward push by the moving air. Airplanes and the wings of birds are designed to force the air more quickly across the top of the wing which gives an upward push called *lift*.

134

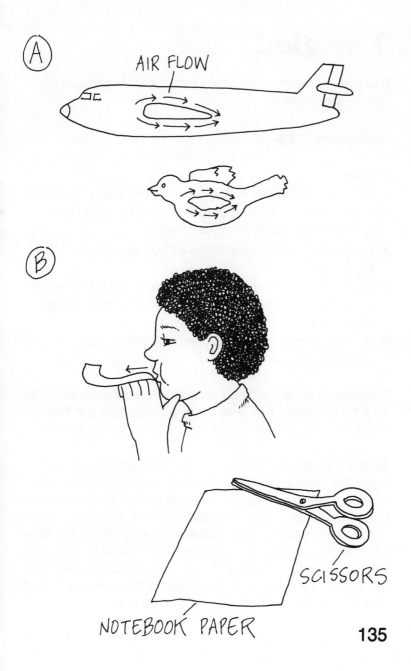

A

AIR FLOW

B

NOTEBOOK PAPER

SCISSORS

135

64. Tangled

Purpose To determine one effect of plastic garbage pollution on sea animals.

Materials *rubberband*

Procedure
- *Hook one end of the rubberband around your little finger.*
- *Stretch the rubberband across the back of your hand and hook the free end on your thumb.*
- *Try to remove the rubberband without touching anything.*
- *Seals and fish do not have hands. How can they remove the plastic rings from six-packs of beverages if they get these around their bodies?*
- *How is the garbage that is dumped in the ocean affecting the sea organisms?*

Results It is very difficult to remove the rubberband from your hand. Seals, fish, and other animals that get tangled with plastic rings find it equally difficult to remove them.

Why? The plastic items in garbage are deadly to sea animals. Turtles swallow floating plastic bags because they mistake them for jellyfish. Their digestive tract becomes blocked and they die. The animals that get plastic rings around their bodies often cannot remove them and they also die. It is still being researched, but it could take as long as 300 years for plastic garbage to decompose in sea water. The trapped animal cannot wait for this. We must take action to prevent the pollution of our oceans.

136

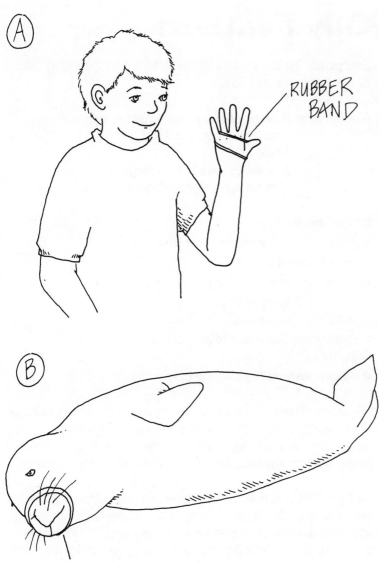

A

RUBBER
BAND

B

PLASTIC RING FROM SODA 6-PACK

137

65. Oily Feathers

Purpose To demonstrate the effect that polluting detergents can have on birds.

Materials *1 quart (1 liter) clear glass bowl*
measuring cup (250 ml)
liquid oil
powdered washing detergent
measuring spoon —teaspoon (5 ml)

Procedure

- *Pour 1 cup of water into the bowl.*
- *Add 1 spoon of liquid oil.*
- *Observe the surface of the water.*
- *Sprinkle 2 spoons of powdered detergent over the surface of the liquid.*
- *Gently stir the water to mix, but try not to produce bubbles.*
- *Again observe the surface of the water.*

Results The oil spread out in large circles on the surface of the water before the addition of the detergent. When the detergent was added, some of the oil sank and the rest broke up into tiny bubbles that covered the water's surface.

Why? Water is heavier and does not mix with oil, thus the oil was able to float on the water's surface. Detergent molecules stick to water on one side and the detergent's opposite side sticks to the oil. The large circles of oil no longer exist because there are molecules of the detergent which allows the oil and water to mix. Detergents can cause a swimming bird to sink and drown. Birds stay afloat because of the oil on their feathers. The birds are waterproof. If the birds become soaked in water containing a high concentration of detergent, the natural oil in the birds' feathers would break up into tiny droplets and allow water to penetrate the feathers. The bird would lose its waterproofing and the extra water on the feathers would increase the bird's weight and it would sink.

66. Pollution

Purpose To observe the outreaching effect of a small amount of pollution on a stream and its wildlife.

Materials *1 gallon (4 liter) glass jar*
measuring cup (250 ml)
red food coloring

Procedure

- *Pour one-half cup of water into the gallon (4 liter) jar.*
- *Add and stir in two drops of food coloring.*
- *Add one cup of water at a time to the jar until the red color disappears.*

Results It takes about 7 measuring cups of clear water to make the red color disappear.

Why? The red is visible at first because the molecules of red color are close enough together to be seen. As clean water is added, the color molecules continue to spread evenly throughout the water. They finally get far enough apart to become invisible because of their small size. This is what happens with some water pollutants. The material may be visible where it is initially dumped, but as it flows downstream and becomes mixed with more water it is no longer seen with the naked eye. This does not mean that it is gone. Just like the red food coloring, it is still in the water and you would be ingesting small quantities if you drank the water. Similarly, animal life in the stream is affected by pollutants many miles from the source.

Ⓐ

RED FOOD COLORING

MEASURING CUP

GALLON JUG

½ CUP RED WATER

Ⓑ

FRESH WATER

141

III

Experiments that Teach Us about Ourselves

The Amazing Human Body

People are biologically similar to other organisms, but we certainly like to consider ourselves different. We think, reason, feel, and respond with much emotion to the world around us. Scientists have learned a great deal about how the human body functions by studying other organisms and comparing how similar materials respond. You will be able to do some of these experimental comparisons as you remove materials from a chicken bone, observe the movement of materials through a semi-permeable membrane similar to a cell membrane, use a water drop to discover how one's eye lens functions, and many more comparison experiments.

This unit also contains experiments that directly study the human body. You will collect fingerprints on cellophane tape, determine your taste sensitivity by eating apple and onion pieces, take your pulse rate with a ball of clay and a paper match, and many more fun experiments.

Studying the human body is a study about yourself. You will barely scratch the surface of all the facts known about the human body, but upon completion of this section you will hopefully know more about yourself than before you started.

67. In But Not Out

Purpose To observe the movement of particles through a membrane.

Materials *1 plastic sandwich bag*
1 twist tie
tincture of iodine
cornstarch
2 measuring cups (500 ml)
eye dropper
measuring spoon—tablespoon (15 ml)

Procedure

■ *Fill a cup one-half full with water, and add 20 drops of iodine.*

■ *Fill a second cup with water and stir in one spoon of cornstarch.*

■ *Pour one-half of the starch and water mixture into the plastic bag.*

■ *Use the twist tie to secure the top of the bag.*

■ *Rinse off any starch and water mixture that might have dropped onto the outside of the bag.*

■ *Place the bag in the cup of water and iodine.*

■ *Observe any changes immediately and then after 30 minutes.*

■ *While waiting for changes to occur inside the bag add 5 drops of iodine to the remaining starch and water mixture in the cup.*

Results The iodine turns the starch and water mixture in the cup black. The iodine does not turn the water in the bowl black, but after a while the contents of the plastic bag turn black.

144

Why? Iodine is used to test for the presence of starch since a purple-black color forms when the two materials are mixed. The water in the bowl never turned black indicating the absence of starch in the water. The iodine particles are small enough to move through the tiny holes in the plastic bag, but the starch molecules are too large to pass through. The inside of the bag turned black because the iodine passed through the membrane and mixed with the starch inside. The water outside contains iodine, but the starch was unable to move out of the bag, thus no color change.

The plastic bag represents a cell membrane with cell parts inside. Materials are able to move into and out of the cell through this membrane. This movement of materials through a membrane is called *osmosis.*

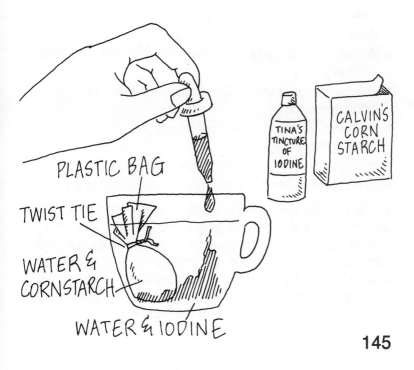

PLASTIC BAG

TWIST TIE

WATER & CORNSTARCH

WATER & IODINE

TINA'S TINCTURE OF IODINE

CALVIN'S CORN STARCH

68. Naked Egg

Purpose To demonstrate the semi-permeability of a cell membrane.

Materials *1 raw egg in its shell*
1 jar with a lid (the egg must fit inside the jar)
clear vinegar
flexible measuring tape

Procedure

- *Measure and record the circumference around the center of the egg.*
- *Record the appearance of the egg.*
- *Place the egg inside the jar.* Do not crack the shell.
- *Cover the egg with vinegar.*
- *Close the lid.*
- *Observe immediately and then periodically for the next 72 hours.*
- *Remove the egg after 72 hours and measure its circumference.*
- *Compare the appearance of the egg before and after being in the vinegar.*
- *How has the egg changed in appearance and size?*
- *Keep the egg for the* Shrinking Egg Experiment 69.

Results The egg has a hard shell on the outside and the circumference will vary. Bubbles start forming on the surface of the egg's shell immediately and increase in number with time. After 72 hours, the shell will be gone and portions of it may be seen floating on the surface of the vinegar. The egg remains intact because of the thin see-through membrane. The size of the egg has increased.

146

Why? The shell of the egg is made of calcium carbonate, commonly called limestone. When vinegar chemically reacts with the limestone, one of the products is carbon dioxide gas, those bubbles seen on the egg. The membrane around the egg does not dissolve in vinegar, but becomes more rubbery. The increased size is due to osmosis, the movement of water through a cell membrane. The water in the vinegar moves through the thin membrane into the egg because the water inside the egg has more materials dissolved in it than does the vinegar. Water will always move through a membrane in the direction where there are more dissolved materials. The contents of the egg stayed inside the membrane because these molecules were too large to pass through the tiny holes. This selectiveness of materials moving through the membrane is called *semi-permeability.*

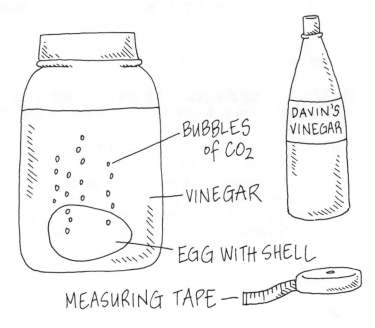

BUBBLES of CO_2

DAVIN'S VINEGAR

VINEGAR

EGG WITH SHELL

MEASURING TAPE

69. Shrinking Egg

Purpose To demonstrate that semi-permeability of a cell membrane.

Materials *egg from Experiment 68 The Naked Egg*
jar with a lid (the egg must fit in the jar)
corn syrup

Procedure
- *Pour 3 inches (7 1/2 cm) of corn syrup into the jar.*
- *Carefully place the egg in the jar.*
- *Close the lid, and allow the jar to stand undisturbed for 72 hours.*
- *Compare the observation of the egg made in Experiment 68 The Naked Egg with its appearance after soaking in the syrup.*
- *What caused the change?*

Results The egg drastically changes in size and shape. It has a rubbery outer skin with very little inside content.

Why? The excess water inside the egg moves through the membrane into the syrup. The water content outside the egg is much less than inside, thus the water moves out of the egg. The molecules in the syrup and other materials inside the egg do not move through the membrane because they are too large. This selectiveness of materials moving through the membrane is called *semi-permeability.*

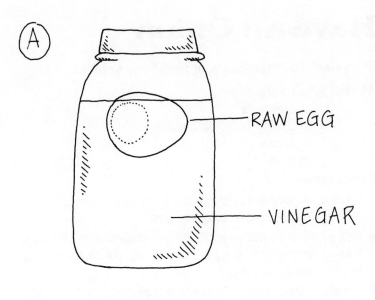

A

RAW EGG

VINEGAR

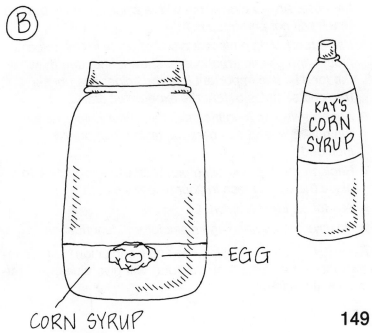

B

KAY'S
CORN
SYRUP

EGG

CORN SYRUP

149

70. Have an Onion

Purpose To determine your sensitivity to taste.

Materials *toothpicks*
blindfold
spring-type clothespin
apple
onion

Procedure

■ *Have an adult peel and cut the apple and onion into small bite size pieces of equal size.*

■ *Ask a helper to assist you with the experiment. Without seeing or smelling, the person will decide on the identity of the food by taste only.*

■ *Blindfold the helper and place the clothespin on his or her nose. An old clothespin with a weak spring is best so that it will not pinch too tightly.*

■ *Use a toothpick to place a piece of apple in the helper's mouth and give instructions to chew it and identify what the food is. It is important that the helper has not seen the food samples before the experiment starts.*

■ *After making an identification, have your helper remove the nose clip and compare the taste when odor is included.*

■ *Replace the clip and blindfold, then use a toothpick to place the onion piece in your helper's mouth.*

■ *Ask for an identification.*

■ *Remove the clip and again ask for an identification.*

Results Without smelling, the apple and onion have a similar taste. The texture of the food will give clues, but the taste is the same.

150

Why? The tongue has nerve endings that allow one to taste things that are sweet, sour, salty, or bitter. Most of the taste sensations experienced are due to smell. Make a note of how tasteless food seems the next time you have a cold and cannot breathe properly.

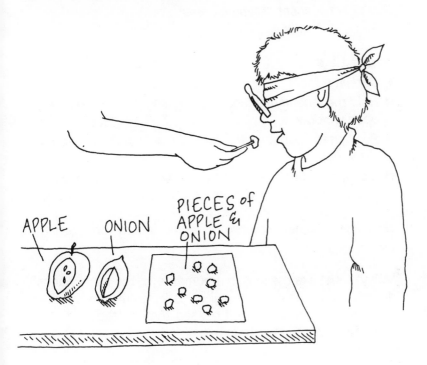

APPLE   ONION   PIECES of APPLE & ONION

71. Eye Lens

Purpose To demonstrate how an eye lens works.

Materials *magnifying lens*
sheet of typing paper
ruler

Procedure
- *Darken a room.*
- *Hold the magnifying lens about 5 feet (1 1/2 m) from an open window*
- *Position the paper on the opposite side of the lens from the window.*
- *Slowly move the paper back and forth from the lens until a clear image of the window and objects outside appear.*

Results A small, colored, inverted image forms on the paper.

Why? Just like the lens in a human eye, the light changes direction as it passes through. The light hits the paper as light hits the retina when it passes through the lens of an eye and forms an inverted image.

152

A

MAGNIFYING LENS

TYPING PAPER

B

RETINA

LENS

72. Finger Monocle

Purpose To make a monocle.

Materials *newspaper*

Procedure
- *Roll one index finger in tightly to form a very tiny hole about the size of the point of a writing pen.*
- *Hold the newspaper close enough to your eyes so that the print is just barely blurred.*
- *Close one eye and with the open eye look through the hole made by your index finger at the blurred newsprint.*

Results The words are less blurred and more readable.

Why? Light reflects off of the newsprint to your eye. As the paper approaches the eye, more light from all directions enters the eye causing the images to appear blurred. The eye pupil closes down to restrict the amount of light, but by covering the eye with the hand, more light can be blocked. The smaller amount of light entering through the tiny hole made by the finger allows a sharper image to be formed on the retina of the eye.

73. Big to Little

Purpose To observe the effect that light has on the size of an eye pupil.

Materials *mirror*

Procedure
- *Sit in a brightly lighted room for two minutes.*
- *Keep one eye tightly closed and the other eye open.*
- *Observe the pupil of the open eye by looking in the mirror. (The pupil is the dark spot in the center of the eye.)*
- *Open the closed eye and immediately observe the size of the pupil.*
- *Notice any size changes in the pupil as the eye remains open.*

Results The pupil in the open eye is very small compared to the pupil of the eye that had been closed. The larger pupil shrinks within seconds after the eye is exposed to the light.

Why? In dim light or darkness, the muscles in the front of the eye relax causing the opening in the eye to enlarge. This hole in the eye is called the pupil, and it regulates the amount of light that enters the eye. In bright light, the opening starts to close thus allowing only a small amount of light to enter the eye. This small hole not only protects the eye from bright light, but improves the image formed on the retina. A sharp image is produced when the extra light is shut out.

157

74. Negative Afterimage

Purpose To experience the effect of tiring the rods and cones in the eye.

Materials   *scissors*
glue
notebook paper
green, black, and orange construction paper

Procedure

- *Use construction paper to make the American Flag, but instead of it being red, white, and blue it will be green, black, and orange.*
- *Alternate green and black strips of paper for the stripes.*
- *The stars are to be black on an orange background.*
- *Glue all the colored pieces to a sheet of notebook paper.*
- *After the flag has been constructed, stare at the center of the flag for one full minute. Make an effort not to move your eyes around and blink as few times as possible.*
- *After the minute of staring, look at a white wall or piece of paper. Blink several times.*

Results The American Flag with its true colors of red, white, and blue seem to appear on the white surface.

Why? On the retina of the eye are light sensitive receivers called cones. They are sensitive to the primary colors of red, blue, and yellow. If a red object is viewed, the red sensitive cones send a message to the brain that the object's color is red. Staring at the green-colored strips stimulates the blue and yellow cones since green is a combination of blue and yellow. Looking at the white paper after tiring the eye stimulates all three kinds of cones equally, but the blue and yellow

158

cones are tired and the red cones send a stronger response. This makes the afterimage appear to be red.

The orange color is a combination of red and yellow so staring at the orange area tires the red and yellow cones. The white light from the paper again stimulates all three cones, but the blue cone sends the strongest response and what was orange produces a blue afterimage.

Very little light is reflected from the black color, thus the cones are not tired when one stares at the black areas. The white light from the white paper stimulates all the cones producing a white afterimage.

75. Wagon Wheel

Purpose To produce the illusion of a moving wagon wheel.

Materials *diagram of circles*

Procedure
- *Hold this book with both hands.*
- *Quickly move the whole book in the smallest possible circular pattern with the center circle as the point of rotation.*

Results The diagram appears to turn like a wagon wheel.

Why? Persistence of vision produces this illusion. The mind retains the image of the drawn circle after it has moved to another position. The retained image plus the real image produce an illusion of motion.

160

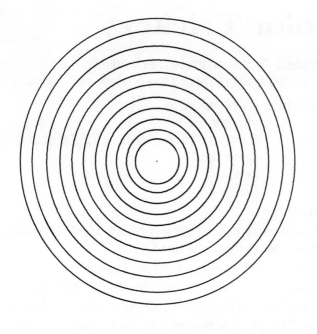

76. Color Trickery

Purpose To demonstrate that it takes different lengths of time for the brain to record the presence of color waves.

Materials *black marker*
straight pin
3 inch × 5 inch (7.6 cm × 12.7 cm) unlined index card
pencil
ruler

Procedure

- *Draw a circle with about a two-inch (5 cm) diameter in the center of the index card.*
- *Reproduce the pattern from the illustrations.*
- *Color the dark sections with the black ink marker.*
- *Push the straight pin through the center of the circle.*
- *Insert the point of the pin into the eraser of the pencil.*
- *Spin the card.*
- *Focus your eyes on a spot just past the rotating circle.*

Results Various combinations of colors appear as the disk rotates. The colors change as the circle changes speed.

Why? The white section of the circle reflects white light, and the black section reflects no light at all. Light is an example of energy. White light contains many colors, and each color has a different amount of energy. The higher the energy content, the faster the color wave travels. It takes time for the eye to receive light waves and then send the message to the brain. As the card spins, only the fastest colors coming from the white section have time to be seen and the message of their arrival sent to the brain before the black section appears.

162

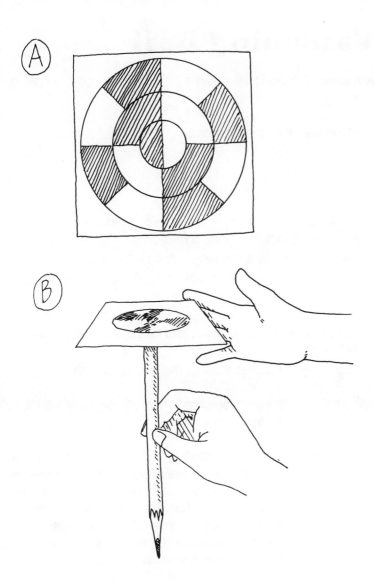

163

77. Vanishing Ball

Purpose To demonstrate the effect of the optic nerve on vision.

Materials *notebook paper*
ruler
pencil

Procedure

■ *In the center of the paper draw two round one-fourth inch (6 mm) colored dots, four inches (10 cm) apart.*

■ *Hold the paper at arms length from your face.*

■ *Close your right eye and look at the dot on the right side with your open eye.*

■ *Slowly move the paper toward your face. Be sure to concentrate on the right dot and* do not *look at the one on the left.*

■ *Stop moving the paper when the left dot vanishes.*

Results The left dot vanishes when the paper is about 1 foot (30 cm) away from your face.

Why? The back of the eyeball is called the retina. Images are directed to this area by the eye's lens and the optic nerve carries the message of the image from the retina to the brain. The optic nerve enters the eyeball at the back and makes a break in the retina. If an image is projected to the spot where the optic nerve enters the retina the image is not seen because no message is sent to the brain. The spot where the optic nerve enters the eye is called the "Blind Spot."

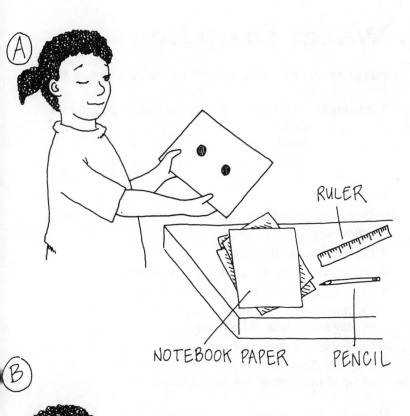

RULER

NOTEBOOK PAPER   PENCIL

165

78. Water Drop Lens

Purpose A water drop is used to simulate an eye lens.

Materials *one 6 inch (15 cm) piece of 20 gauge wire*
pencil
bowl
newspaper

Procedure
- *Twist one end of the wire around the pencil to make a round loop.*
- *Fill the bowl with water.*
- *Dip the wire into the water with the open loop pointing up.*
- *Lift the loop carefully out of the water and hold it over the newspaper. You want a large rounded drop of water to stay in the hole of the wire loop.*
- *Look through the water drop at the letters on the page. You may have to move the loop up and down to find a position that makes the letters clear.*

Results The letters are enlarged. If the letters look smaller dip the loop into the water again.

Why? The water drop is curved outward and acts like a convex lens. This type of lens is used as a magnifying lens and is the type of lens in eyes. Sometimes the water drop stretches so tightly between the wire that it curves downward forming a concave lens. This type of lens causes the letters to look small.

166

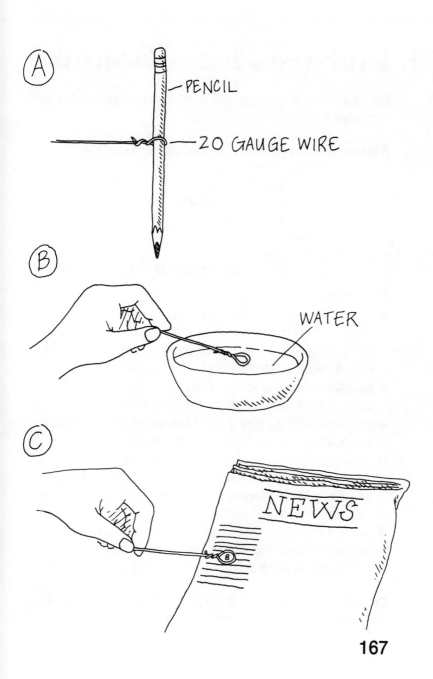

79. Pictures from Sound

Purpose To show that the mind can change sound messages into mental pictures.

Materials *4 cardboard school boxes (cigar boxes will work)*
4 marbles
sheet of poster board
masking tape
marker
scissors
2 small boxes that will fit inside a school box

Procedure
- *Cut two strips from the poster board, one must fit diagonally across the inside of a school box and the other must fit across the box. Be sure the lid of the box will close when these strips are in position.*
- *Label one box 1 and tape the paper strip diagonally across. Add one marble and tape the box closed.*
- *Label the second box 2 and tape the paper strip across the box. Add one marble and tape the box closed.*
- *The remaining school boxes are to be labeled 3 and 4. The small boxes are to be taped inside the school boxes as shown in the diagram. Add one marble to each box and tape the lids closed.*
- *Ask a helper to rotate each box back and forth and determine from the sounds heard the shape of the open space inside each box.*

Results The sound of the rolling marble allows the helper to determine the inside structure of the box.

Why? As the marble moves around, mental notes are made of the length of time before it hits something. When enough information is put together a mental picture of the inside of each box is formed.

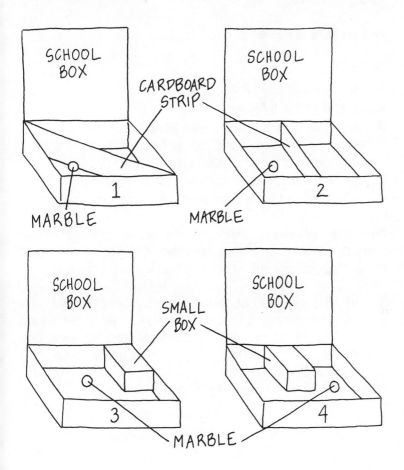

80. Sound and Direction

Purpose To test one's ability to determine the direction of a sound source.

Materials *a helper*

Procedure
- *Have a helper sit in a chair.*
- *Tell him to close his eyes.*
- *Snap your fingers above his head and have him determine the area, front, top, or back of his head that you snap your fingers.* Note: *Be sure your fingers are held an equal distance between your helper's ears.*
- *Do this several times changing the snapping position.*

Results By random chance, some of the answers will be correct, but if enough trials are made it will be obvious that the person cannot tell where the sound is coming from.

Why? The direction of sound is not always clear unless it is coming from a point directed toward the ear. If the sound is in the center of the head at the front, top, or back, one cannot tell the exact direction of the sound source. This confusion is due to the fact that in these areas the sound is received with equal intensity by both ears.

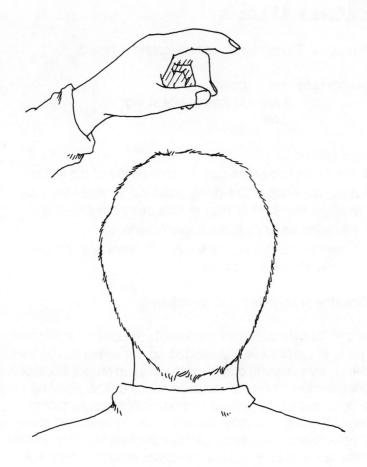

171

81. Hearing

Purpose To demonstrate how sound is heard.

Materials *metal spoon*
2 feet (61 cm) of kite string
ruler

Procedure
- *Tie the handle of the spoon in the center of the string.*
- *Wrap the ends of the string around both index fingers. Be sure that both strings are the same length.*
- *Place the tip of an index finger in each ear.*
- *Lean over so that the spoon hangs freely and tap it against the side of a table.*

Results It sounds like a church bell.

Why? The metal in the spoon starts to vibrate when struck. These vibrations are transmitted up the string to the ears. The ability to hear is due to one's ability to detect vibrations. Objects must vibrate to produce a sound. The vibrating objects causes the air around it to move. Vibrating air molecules enters the ear and strike the ear drum causing it to vibrate. These vibrations continue to travel through bones and fluids in the ear until they reach a nerve that sends the message to the brain.

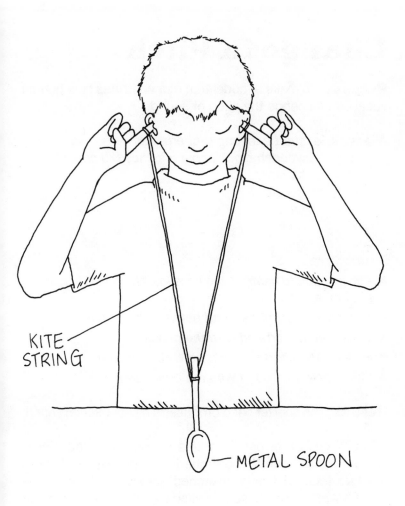

KITE
STRING

METAL SPOON

173

82. Change in Pitch

Purpose To make a model that demonstrates how human vocal cords change the pitch of sound.

Materials *short and long rubberbands*
wooden block about 8 inches (20 cm) long
hammer
2 nails
pencil
ruler

Procedure

- *Ask an adult to hammer the nails into the board 6 inches (15 cm) apart.*
- *Stretch a short rubberband between the two nails.*
- *Pluck the rubberband with the pencil.*
- *Replace the short rubberband with a long one.*
- *Pluck the rubberband with the pencil as before.*

Results The shorter band produces a higher pitched sound.

Why? The tighter band vibrates faster, thus producing a higher pitched sound. The rubberbands behave similarly to the two folds of tissue stretched across the larynx, "the Adam's Apple." This tissue is called the vocal cord. When air strums these cords they vibrate. The pitch of the sound varies as the tension changes. When the cords relax, they vibrate slowly and the pitch is lower than when the cords are tightened.

174

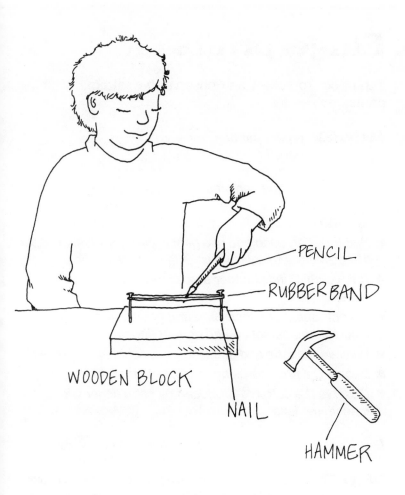

PENCIL

RUBBER BAND

WOODEN BLOCK

NAIL

HAMMER

175

83. Fingerprints

Purpose To collect and observe the patterns of finger prints.

Materials *typing paper*
pencil
clear tape
magnifying lens

Procedure

■ *Rub the sharpened end of a pencil across a sheet of paper 15 to 20 times to collect a layer of graphite on the paper.*

■ *Rub your left index finger across the graphite on the paper.*

■ *Tear off about one inch (2 1/2 cm) of clear tape and stick it across the darkened end of your finger.*

■ *Remove the tape and stick it on a sheet of typing paper.*

■ *Repeat the process using the tips of other fingers.*

■ *Observe the patterns produced by each finger with a magnifying lens.*

Results The patterns on each fingerprint is the same.

Why? The inner layer of skin called the dermis has projections. The outer skin layer, the epidermis, fits over these projections, thus taking on the same pattern. It has been observed that each person has a fingerprint unique to that individual. These personal signatures form five months before birth and never change.

176

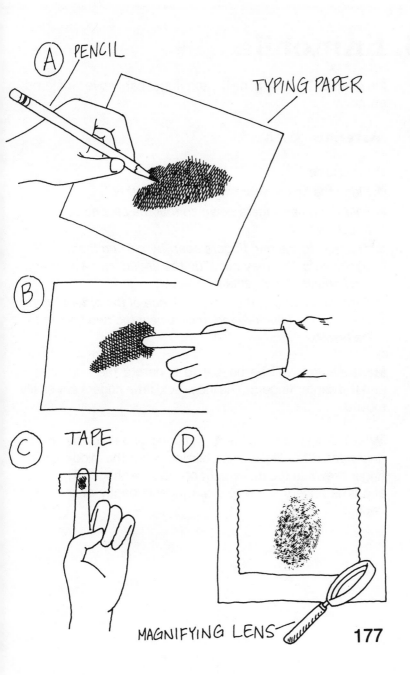

A. PENCIL

TYPING PAPER

B.

C. TAPE

D.

MAGNIFYING LENS

177

84. Immobile

Purpose To determine if each finger can move independently.

Materials *your hands*

Procedure
- *Place the tips of your ring fingers together.*
- *Fold the other fingers down so that the second set of knuckles touch.*
- *Try moving the ring fingers apart by moving them backwards. You may not slide the fingers sideways and the knuckles must remain together.*
- *Experiment to test the independence of the other fingers. Place all the knuckles together except the two fingers to be tested.*

Results You will be unable to separate the ring fingers and the center fingers. The index and little fingers are easily moved.

Why? A ligament connects the ring finger to the middle finger and other digits. Immobilizing either the middle or ring finger prevents the movement of the other finger. The index and little fingers seem to work independently of the other fingers.

178

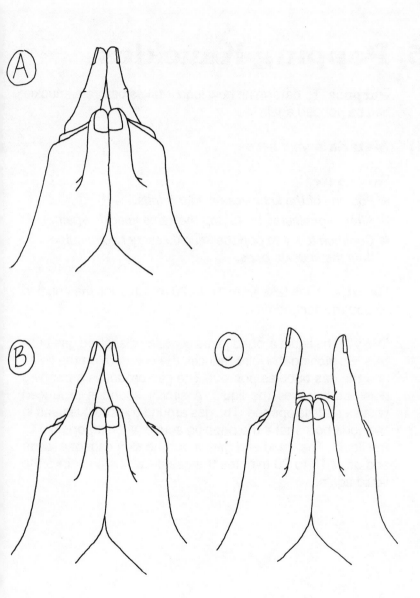

179

85. Popping Knuckles

Purpose To determine how long it takes before a knuckle can be popped again.

Materials *your hand*

Procedure
- *Pop one of the knuckles on your hands.*
- *After two minutes try to pop the same knuckle again.*
- *Continue to try to pop the knuckle every two minutes until the knuckle pops.*

Results It will take from 10 to 20 minutes for the knuckle to pop the second time.

Why? The liquid around joints contains dissolved gas bubbles. Stretching the joint reduces the pressure on the liquid and the gas bubbles pop out. The gas produces a popping noise as it leaves the liquid. A similar sound is produced when a soda is opened. The gas around the knuckles and in the soda both make the popping sound when it pops out of the liquid. The liquid and gas under the skin cannot escape and after 10 to 20 minutes the gas dissolves back into the liquid again.

180

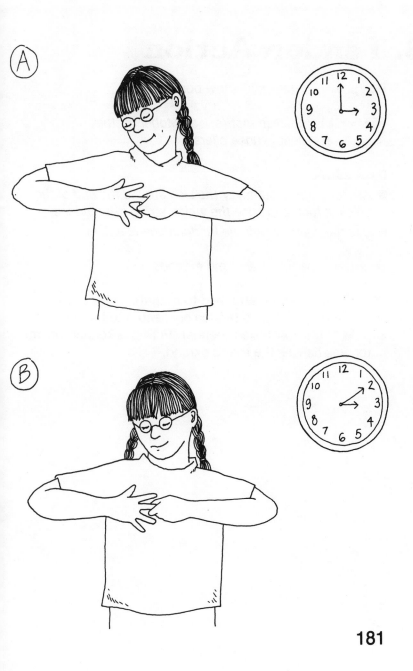

181

86. Tendon Action

Purpose To determine how bones move.

Materials *chicken foot (ask a butcher for this)*
needle nose pliers

Procedure
- *Ask an adult to cut away the skin around the end of the chicken foot to expose the white, string-like tendons.*
- *Use the pliers to pull the tendons one at a time.*

Results The toes bend and extend.

Why? Tendons are attached to both the outer and under-side of the toe. When a tendon connected to the underside is pulled, the toe flexes (bends). Pulling a tendon on the outer side causes the toe to extend.

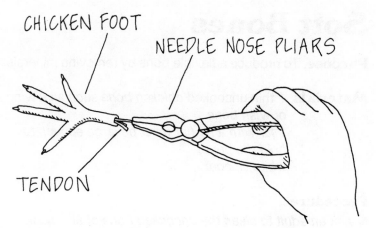

CHICKEN FOOT

NEEDLE NOSE PLIARS

TENDON

87. Soft Bones

Purpose To produce a flexible bone by removing minerals.

Materials *1* thin uncooked *chicken bone such as a wing or wish bone*
1 jar with a lid (jar must be large enough to hold the bone)
white vinegar

Procedure

- *Ask an adult to clean the uncooked bone of all muscles and tendons.*
- *Allow the bone to dry overnight.*
- *Place the bone in the jar. Add enough vinegar to cover the bone.*
- *Secure the lid and allow the jar to stand undisturbed for 7 days.*
- *Remove the bone and rinse with water.*
- *Test the flexibility of the bone daily by bending it back and forth with your fingers.*

Results The ends of the bone become soft first. As time passes the bone starts to soften toward the center. The final result is a soft rubbery bone that can be twisted.

Why? Minerals in the bone cause it to be strong and rigid. The vinegar removes these minerals from the bone leaving it soft and pliable.

184

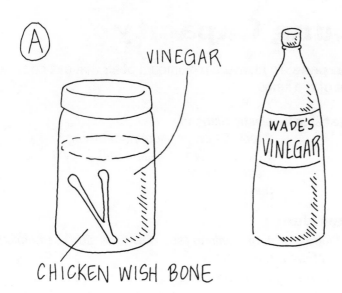

A

VINEGAR

WADE'S VINEGAR

CHICKEN WISH BONE

B

185

88. Lung Capacity

Purpose To measure the amount of air that can be forced out of the lungs.

Materials *plastic dishpan*
2 feet (61 cm) of aquarium tubing
1 gallon (4 liters) plastic milk jug with cap
masking tape
pen

Procedure

- *Place a strip of masking tape down the side of the milk jug from top to bottom.*
- *Fill the jug with water, and screw on the cap.*
- *Fill the dishpan about 1/2 full with water.*
- *Place the jug upside down in the water, and remove the cap.*
- *Have a helper hold the jug. DO NOT allow air bubbles to enter the milk jug.*
- *Place one end of the aquarium tubing inside the mouth of the jug.*
- *Take a normal breath and exhale through the tubing. Mark the water level on the tape.*
- *Refill the jug with water and return it to the dishpan.*
- *Breath in deeply and make an effort to exhale all of the air out of your lungs through the tubing. Mark the water level on the tape.*

Results The water level drops as exhaled air enters the jug. Normal breathing does not push out as much water as does deep breathing.

186

Why? When the air enters the jug it pushes the water out the opening. In normal breathing, only about one eighth of the lungs' capacity is used. During exercise, more air is taken in and exhaled, thus there is a larger amount of air exhaled during deep breathing.

(A)

MILK JUG

MASKING TAPE

(B)

AQUARIUM TUBING

PLASTIC DISHPAN

PEN

89. Heartbeat

Purpose To observe the vibration of a match due to the pulsation of blood in the wrist.

Materials *modeling clay*
paper
match

Procedure

- *Insert the match into a very small piece of clay (the smaller the better).*
- *Flatten the bottom of the clay.*
- *Place your wrist, palm side up, on a table.*
- *Place the clay on your wrist, and move the clay around on the thumb side of the wrist until the match starts to slowly vibrate back and forth.*
- *Count the number of vibrations that the match makes in one minute.*

Results The match vibrates back and forth with a regular beat. For adults it will vibrate 60 to 80 times in one minute. The vibration for children is from 80 to 140 beats per minute.

Why? As the heart contracts, blood is forced through the blood vessels. The blood moves at a rhythmic rate causing the blood vessels in the wrist to pulsate. All blood vessels have this throbbing motion, but the vessels in the wrist are close to the surface of the skin and can be felt more easily. The movement of the blood under the clay causes it and the match to vibrate.

188

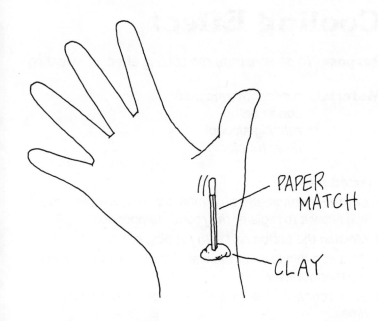

PAPER
MATCH

CLAY

189

90. Cooling Effect

Purpose To demonstrate the cooling effect of sweating.

Materials *outdoor thermometer*
cotton ball
rubbing alcohol
timer (or clock)

Procedure

- *Lay the thermometer on a table for three minutes; this will allow it to register the room's temperature.*
- *Moisten the cotton ball with rubbing alcohol.*
- *Spread a thin layer of the wet cotton across the bulb of the thermometer.*
- *Blow your breath across the wet cotton about fifteen times.*

Results Blowing on the wet cotton causes the thermometer to record a lower temperature.

Why? The cooling effect of the alcohol is due to the evaporation of the liquid around the thermometer bulb. Evaporation occurs when a liquid absorbs enough heat energy to change from a liquid to a gas. The evaporating alcohol takes energy away from the mercury in the thermometer bulb causing the mercury to cool. The cooled mercury contracts and moves down the column in the thermometer. During warm weather, sweat glands release more liquids on the surface of the skin. This process is commonly called sweating. As the sweat evaporates, it removes heat from the skin causing the skin to feel cooler.

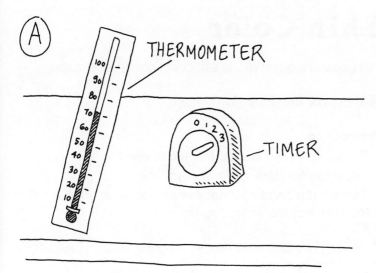

(A) THERMOMETER

TIMER

RUSSELL'S RUBBING ALCOHOL

THERMOMETER

COTTON BALL

91. Skin Color

Purpose To observe the effect of light on skin color.

Materials *band-aid*

Procedure
- *Place a band-aid around the end of one finger.*
- *Leave the bandage on for 2 days.*
- *Remove the band-aid bandage and observe the color of the skin over the entire finger.*

Results The skin color is much lighter where it was covered by the bandage.

Why? Special cells in animals contain dark brown grains called melanin. In the absence of light, the grains group together producing skin with a light appearance. Melanin responds to light by spreading out causing the skin to be much darker. People with dark skin have more melanin. Albinos have no melanin in their skin. The skin of albinos is white.

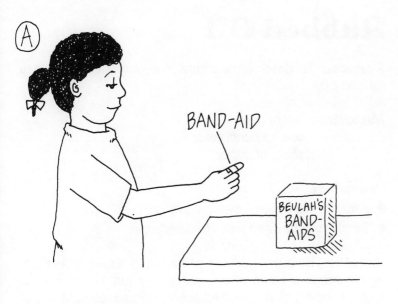

BAND-AID

193

92. Rubbed Off

Purpose To demonstrate how the epidermal cells are rubbed off.

Materials *bar of soap*
course sandpaper
sheet of paper

Procedure
- *Hold the bar of soap over the paper.*
- *Gently rub the soap with the sandpaper.*

Results The outer surface of the soap bar is rubbed off by the rough surface of the sandpaper just like the outer layer of human skin is rubbed away by rough objects.

Why? The outer layer of human skin, the epidermis, like the soap is constantly rubbed off, but unlike the soap human cells are replaced. We live in a world that constantly rubs, scraps, grinds, cuts, and pushes against our skin. The outer layer is composed of dead cells that just fall off when touched. The body does not wear away as the soap did because there is a constant replacement of these lost cells by the under layer of cells. When cut, the cells grow back together. The epidermis is constantly changing and repairing itself.

194

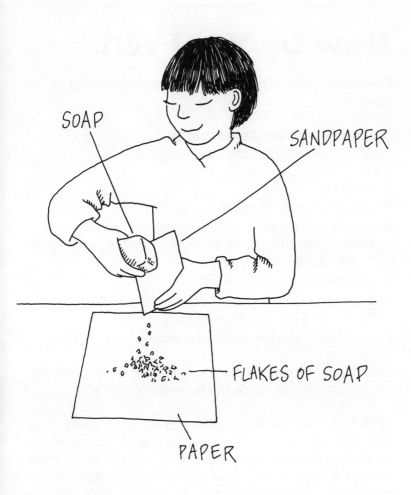

SOAP

SANDPAPER

FLAKES OF SOAP

PAPER

93. How Do You Feel?

Purpose To test the sensitivity of different parts of the skin.

Materials *two sharpened pencils*
masking tape

Procedure

- *Tape the pencils together so that the points are even.*
- *Ask a helper to look away as you gently touch his forearm with both pencil points. Be sure the points touch the skin at the same time.*
- *Ask how many points are felt.*
- *Do the experiment again, but touch the pencil points to the tip of the helper's thumb or finger.*
- *Again ask how many points are felt.*

Results The person feels only one point on the forearm, and two points are felt on the finger or thumb tip.

Why? The nerve endings in the arm and other parts of the body are too few in number to allow one to distinguish the separate pressures from the pencil points. The extra number of nerve endings in the finger and thumb tips allows one to make more accurate identifications. There is an increase in the pain experienced in areas with more nerve endings.

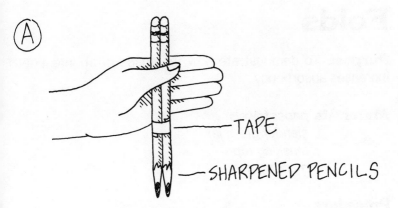

TAPE

SHARPENED PENCILS

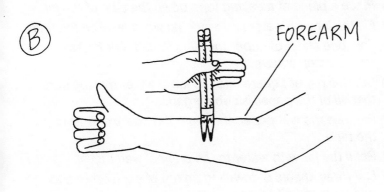

FOREARM

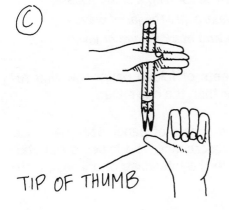

TIP OF THUMB

94. Folds

Purpose To demonstrate how the shape of an intestine increases absorbency.

Materials *paper towels*
slender glass jar
masking tape
marking pen

Procedure

- *Place a piece of masking tape down the side of the jar.*
- *Fill the jar with water and mark the water level on the tape.*
- *Fold one sheet of paper toweling in half four times to form a small square.*
- *Dip this paper square into the jar of water making sure that all of the paper is submerged.*
- *Remove the wet paper and mark the new water level on the tape.*
- *Refill the jar with water to the original water level.*
- *Lay three sheets of toweling on top of each other and fold them in half four times forming a small square.*
- *Dip the entire paper square into the jar of water.*
- *Remove the wet paper and mark the water level.*

Results The three sheets of folded paper toweling removed much more water than the one sheet.

Why? Folding the three sheets of paper does decrease their size, but not their absorbency. The folded sheets behave like the tissue inside the intestines of animals. Both have the ability to absorb large quantities of liquid because of their cellular makeup and because of their available surface area. The human intestine provides a large absorbing surface because not only is the coiled tube about 20 feet (6 m) long, but its inside walls are lined with fold after fold of soft absorbing tissue.

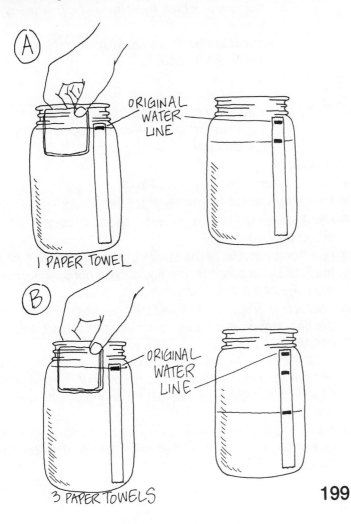

(A) ORIGINAL WATER LINE

1 PAPER TOWEL

(B) ORIGINAL WATER LINE

3 PAPER TOWELS

95. Small Intestine

Purpose To demonstrate the movement of soluble materials through the lining of the small intestine.

Materials   *sugar*
cornstarch
tincture of iodine (purchase at a pharmacy)
funnel
round coffee filters (large enough to fit inside the funnel)
1 glass jar
1 small drinking glass
1 measuring cup (250 ml)
1 measuring spoon —tablespoon (15 ml)
eye dropper

Procedure

- *Line the funnel with 5 coffee filters.*
- *Place the stem of the funnel in the jar.*
- *Mix 1 spoon of cornstarch and 1 spoon of sugar with one cup of water.*
- *Pour three fourths of the starch and water solution into the funnel. Be sure that the liquid does not spill over the top edge of the funnel into the jar.*
- *Pour a few drops of the liquid that has passed through the filter paper into a small drinking glass. Taste this colorless liquid.*
  Note: Never taste anything in a laboratory setting unless you are sure that it contains no harmful chemicals. This experiment is safe since the liquid only contains water and sugar.
- *Add 3 drops of tincture of iodine to the remaining liquid that passed through the filter paper. DO NOT taste. Note the color produced.*

200

■ Add 3 drops of tincture of iodine to the remaining starch, sugar, and water solution in the cup. Note the color.

Results The sugar, starch, and water solution turns a purple-black color when the tincture of iodine is added. The liquid that passed through the filter paper tastes sweet and turns a pale amber color with no shades of purple when the iodine is added.

Why? Iodine is used to test for the presence of starch. A purple color results when iodine and starch combine. The lack of a purple color in the liquid that passed through the filter paper indicates that starch did not pass through the paper. The lining of the small intestine like the filter paper allows small molecules to pass through, but the large starch molecules cannot get through the small holes in the paper or the intestine lining. The sugar, sucrose, used in this experiment is small enough to pass through the filter paper and it is a much larger molecule than glucose, the sugar that passes through the intestine lining.

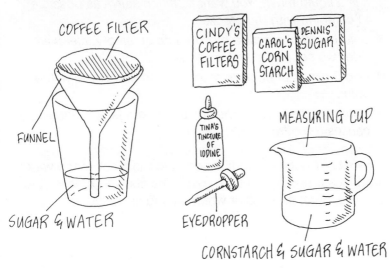

96. Size Change

Purpose To determine if some digestion occurs in the mouth.

Materials *saltine cracker*
tincture of iodine (purchase at a pharmacy)
eye dropper
2 small jars
measuring spoon — tablespoon (15 ml)

Procedure

- *Break the cracker in half.*
- *Crumble one half of the cracker into a clean jar.*
- *Add 2 spoons of water to the jar containing the cracker and stir well.*
- *Add 3 drops of tincture of iodine and stir. Observe the color.*
- *Chew the remaining piece of cracker for 1 minute or until it is a liquid mush. You want as much saliva as possible to combine with the cracker.*
- *Spit the cracker-saliva mixture into an empty, clean jar. Add two spoons of water and stir.*
- *Add 3 drops of tincture of iodine and stir. Observe the color.*
- *Compare the color of the liquids in both jars. What causes the difference?*

Results Tincture of iodine added to the cracker and water produces a purple to black color. The chewed cracker produces a much paler color when the iodine is added.

Why? Iodine is used to test for the presence of starch. Any starchy substance will turn purple when touched by iodine. Chewing the cracker mixes it with saliva. Chemicals called enzymes in saliva change starch molecules into a sugar called glucose. Iodine has no effect on glucose thus the color of the chewed cracker plus iodine is a pale purple because most of the starch has been changed to glucose. This change of starch to glucose is part of the digestive process and this experiment demonstrates that digestion does occur in the mouth.

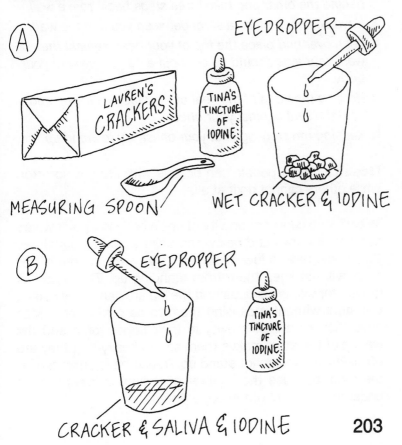

97. Who Can?

Purpose The difference in the position of center of gravity in males and females is demonstrated.

Materials *short stool*

Procedure
- *Stand with tips of shoes touching a wall. Place one foot behind the other and take three steps back from a wall.*
- *Have someone place a stool between you and the wall.*
- *Lean over and place the top of your head against the wall. Your legs should be at about a 45° angle with your body.*
- *Holding the edge of the seat of the stool, pick it up and hold the seat against your chest.*
- *Keeping the stool against your chest, try to stand up.*

Results Some people can do this with little or no effort while others cannot do it at all.

Why? The center of gravity of one's body is a point where the weight above and below the point would be equal. For those who have a low center of gravity, the weight of the stool will not keep them from standing up. The center of gravity for women is usually in the hip area and they can lift the stool without it causing them to be off balance. Men have their center of gravity in their upper torso and the weight of the stool makes them so top heavy that they are off balance and cannot stand up. Young boys often can lift the stool because their center of gravity is lower due to underdevelopment of the upper torso.

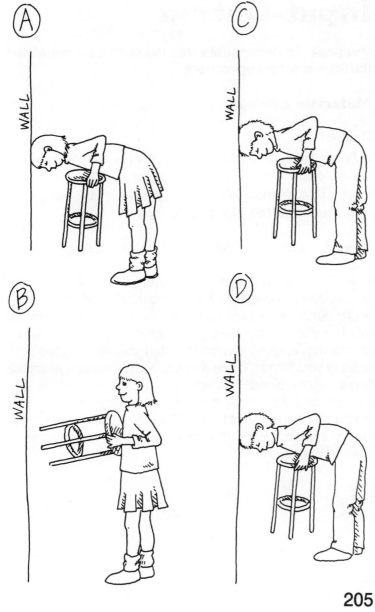

98. Input-Output

Purpose To demonstrate that the output message from the brain is not always correct.

Materials *a partner*

Procedure

■ *Place the palm of your hand against the palm of your partner's.*

■ *With your thumb and index finger of your free hand, rub the outside of the joined index fingers.*

Results It feels as if part of your finger is asleep.

Why? The brain is like a computer, and it contains programs. When you rub your finger, both sides of the touched finger sends messages to the brain. The finger doing the rubbing also sends messages. These messages are paired up and the resulting sensation is that you have rubbed both sides of your finger. There was a missing message when the fingers were joined with your partner. This touching was inputed, and the output message was that there is no feeling on one side of your finger. The brain takes in and feeds out information. Even though we know better, we cannot change the output.

207

99. Spinning

Purpose To demonstrate the effects of spinning the body around rapidly.

Materials *yourself*

Procedure
- *Position yourself outdoors in an open area.*
- *Turn around rapidly five times.*
- *Sit on the ground.*

Results You will feel dizzy for a short time after you have stopped turning.

Why? The liquid in the canals of the ear begins to move as the body turns. When the body stops revolving, the liquid continues to turn, and this motion is interpreted by the brain to mean the body is still turning.

100. Change of Pattern

Purpose To test one's power of concentration.

Materials *a partner*

Procedure
- *Ask your partner to pat the top of his head with one hand and to pat his stomach with the other hand.*
- *Have him to continue patting the head, but to start rubbing the stomach in a circular motion.*
- *Reverse the movements and have your partner rub his head while patting his stomach.*

Results It is easy for the hands to perform the same pattern of movement, but much concentration is necessary to successfully move the hands simultaneously in two different patterns.

Why? Through repetition of motion one becomes proficient at moving the hands in the same pattern. One's brain is programmed to do this. Back-and-forth motions or circular motions are easily done, but only one pattern at a time. Both types of motion are in the brain's many programs, but it takes much concentration to activate the two programs at the same time.

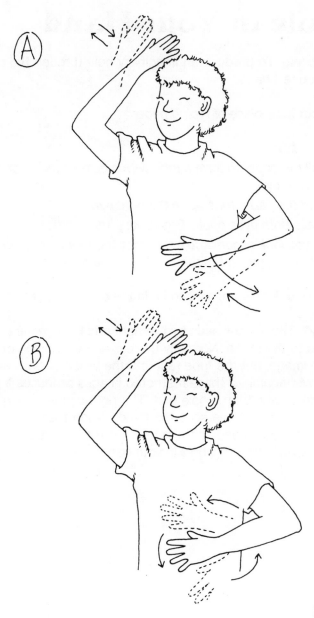

211

101. Hole in Your Hand

Purpose To produce an imaginary hole through the center of one's hand.

Materials *piece of typing paper*

Procedure
- *Roll the paper to form a tube with a hole about as large as your eye.*
- *Hold the paper tube up to the right eye.*
- *Leave both eyes open.* This is very important.
- *As you look at some object across the room place your left hand against the tube with your palm facing you.*

Results A hole appears to be in the palm of your hand.

Why? The images seen by the right and left eyes are projected to the retina. Normally there is an overlapping of the same image, but the tube restricts the vision of both eyes. The overlapping of these restricted images produces a picture of a hand with a hole in it. The right eye is seeing the tube and the left eye sees the hand. When these two pictures are overlapped on the retina, the message sent to the brain is that there is a hole in your hand.

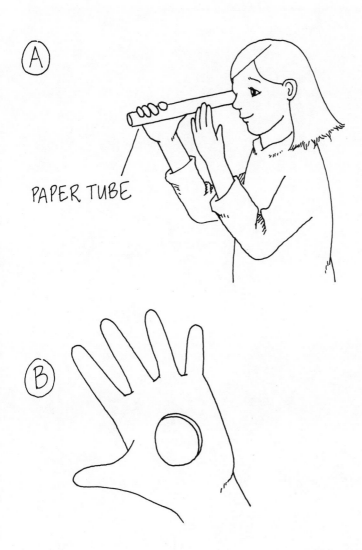

A

PAPER TUBE

B

213

Glossary

Adam's Apple: The larynx or voice box.

Albino: Skin without color due to the lack of melanin.

Auxin: A chemical that changes the speed of plant growth.

Behavior: Activity of a living organism.

Bioluminescence: Light produced by living organisms.

Blind Spot: Where the optic nerve enters the eye.

Brine: Salt.

Camouflage: When the color of an organism blends into that of its environment making the organism difficult to find.

Carotenoid: Plant pigment used in photosynthesis; its color ranges from red to yellow.

Casts: Undigested soil deposited by earthworms.

Cell Membrane: A thin skin-like structure around the outside of cells.

Center of Gravity: The point at which the weight of an object is equally distributed. The object will balance at this point.

215

Chlorophyll: The green pigment that plants use in the energy reaction called photosynthesis.

Chromatography: The word means to write with color. It is a method of separating mixtures.

Cones: Light sensitive receivers on the retina; allows one to see color.

Cytoplasm: A jelly-like material in cells. The living part of the cell.

Dehydration: Movement of water out of a cell.

Dermis: The inner layer of the skin.

Diffusion: Spontaneous movement of molecules from one place to another resulting in a uniform mixture.

Epicotyl: Part of a seed that forms the leaves.

Epidermis: Outer layer of skin.

Evaporation: The change of liquid water into gas.

Expiration: When air moves out of the lungs.

Fungus: A protist that has both plant and animal characteristics. Fungi means food-robbing.

Hilum: Scar on a bean where it had been attached to the bean pod wall.

Hypocotyl: Part of a seed that forms the stem.

Indicator: Solution used to test for the presence of an acid or base.

Larvae: The worm-like stage in insect development after the egg.

Larynx: Voice box.

216

Lens: Transparent disk in the eye that directs images to the retina.

Lift: The upward push on flying objects.

Ligament: A tough strand-like tissue that holds joints together.

Luciferin: A chemical in some organisms that gives off light when combined with oxygen.

Luminescence: Light that is not produced by heating an object.

Melanin: Special cells containing dark grains which produce skin color.

Micropyle: Small opening through which pollen grains enter a seed.

Mold: A form of fungus.

Optic Nerve: Large nerve leading from the back of the eyeball to the vision center in the brain.

Osmosis: The movement of a material such as water from an area of great amounts of water to an area of lesser amounts of water.

Penicillin: Greenish mold found on food; used to make medicine. Word penicillus means paint brush. The name penicillin was given to the mold because it looks like a brush.

Phototropism: Plant growth in response to light.

Photosynthesis: Energy-making reaction in plants. It uses carbon dioxide, water, and sunlight to produce oxygen, sugar, and energy.

Pulse: Throbbing movement in blood vessels.

Pupa: The stage of insect development after the larvae stage.

Pupil: Opening in the front of the eye through which light passes.

Radicle: Part of a seed that forms the root.

Respiration: A reaction in plants and animals that uses oxygen and sugar to produce carbon dioxide, water, and energy.

Retina: Back layer of the eyeball where images are focused by the lens.

Seed Coat: Protective covering on a seed.

Semi-permeable Membrane: A material that allows different sized materials to pass through it.

Spore: A reproductive cell in some organisms such as mold.

Stomata: Pores in plant leaves.

Sweating: Evaporation of liquid from the skin.

Tendon: Fibrous tissue that connects a muscle to a bone.

Transpiration: Loss of water through plant pores, the stomata.

Tuber: An underground stem.

Turgor Pressure: Pressure of water inside cells.

Vocal Cord: Tissue stretched across the larynx.

Xylem: Tiny tubes in the stalk of a plant stem; transports water and food to the plant cells.

Index

220

221